Dingers!

a division of

DING

by Peter Keating

ESPN BOOKS

BOOK DESIGN: SpotCo; Sam Eckersley, Bashan Aquart, Tzvetan Kostov

RESEARCH: Simon Brennan, Doug Mittler

EDITOR: Glen Waggoner

COPY EDITOR: Beth Adelman

ISBN: 1-933060-09-3

ESPN books are available for special promotions and
premiums. For details contact Michael Rentas, Assistant
Director, Inventory Operations, Hyperion, 77 West 66th St., 11th
floor, New York, NY 10023, or call 212-456-0133.

FIRST EDITION

10 9 8 7 6 5 4 3 2 1

For Karen, the shot heard 'round my world.

No one can understand

what it really is unless you have felt it in your own hands and body. It is different from seeing it or trying to describe it. There is nothing I know quite like meeting a ball in exactly the right spot. As the ball makes its high, long arc beyond the playing field, the diamond and the stands suddenly belong to one man. In that brief, brief time, you are free of all demands and complications. There is no one behind you, no obstruction ahead, as you follow this clear path all around the bases. This is the batsman's center stage, the one time that he may allow himself to freely accept the limelight, to enjoy the sensation of every eye in the stadium fixed on him, waiting for the moment when his foot will touch home plate. In this moment, he is free.

— Sadaharu Oh

LEADING OFF

A Short History of the Long Ball

CONTENTS

Leading Off

Talking baseball

always involves tall tales—doubly so when conversations revolve around the heroic act of hitting a home run, and quadruply so when the events being discussed took place in the distant past.

A lot of the fun in putting together a book like this consists of figuring out which stories are true (Nelson Barrera really did die touching a high-voltage cable when he was just five homers short of the all-time minor league record) and which aren't (Mickey Mantle's dingers didn't really travel 700 feet), all the while picking up new and fascinating information along the way.

But there's one quote I have come across that I didn't check because I don't want to know if it's true. It is statement attributed, on dozens of Internet sites, among other places, to Hank Aaron:

"I still think the triple is the most exciting thing in baseball. To me, a triple is like a guy taking the ball on his 1-yard line and running 99 yards for a touchdown."

Now, I have always been an Aaron fan, and in researching this book over the past year,

I have come to admire him deeply. His sustained excellence and the grace with which he handled unimaginable pressure as he pursued Babe Ruth's career home run record weren't just expressions of his dignity—they were also gifts to the rest of us. And his book, *I Had a Hammer,* (written with Lonnie Wheeler) is one of the best sports autobiographies of all time.

But I'm not going to Google that quote or look it up in LexisNexis or call Aaron about it, because if the all-time home run king really thinks triples are the most exciting play in baseball, I'd have to pick a fight with him.

I mean, when *The Sporting News* chose the 25 greatest moments in baseball history, 13 of them—including six of the top seven—were home runs. How many great triples have you seen recently?

Even if you love to watch a ball bouncing around the far reaches of the outfield without going over the wall while runners scoot around the bases, a triple still isn't the most exciting play in baseball. An inside-the-park home run is.

But that's not really the point.

What triples advocates are really saying is that they prefer speed to power, and that hitting at its best is really about the construction, as opposed to the production, of runs. They're saying that singles and stolen bases and ground balls to the right side of the infield in all their small-ball glory are the apotheosis of team play. After all, what would be more wonderful than a player, having tripled, to score on a sacrifice fly, or, better yet, a squeeze play!

Well, technically a home run would be more wonderful because it would consume fewer outs, but traditionalists don't worry too much about outs. That's why they end up watching and pretending to love so many 2-1 ballgames. When your favorite players are moving runners over instead of getting on base, your favorite team's not going to put too many runs on the scoreboard.

Beyond that, members of the life-is-speed-and-sacrifices crowd always give off the whiff that they feel home runs are so ... unsophisticated. And to a certain extent, they're right.

Although baseball is a game, it's not supposed to be easy. And when a big palooka steps off a farm and starts knocking balls out of bandboxes, he's not honoring the delicate rhythms of the game, the taut balance between batter and pitcher. And he's injuring the cherished notion that ballplayers have to apprentice with old masters to learn how to round and refine their skills.

So what? Should the violation of 19th-century customs have been enough for Mickey Mantle to be booed for the first 600 games of his career, when he was the best player in baseball and his team was winning the World Series almost every year?

Hitting a home run is the single most important thing a player can do to win games. The ability to hit home runs is the single most important skill a player can have. And when players bring that talent to bear, the quality of games improves.

Of course, home run hitting can go too far. Unless you're a Giants fanatic, it's fairly boring to watch the way the fear of Barry Bonds' power has reduced his plate appearances to a series of intentional walks punctuated by mammoth blasts. But it's the injection of danger, the idea that any at-bat might turn the world upside-down, that brought life to deadball and made baseball a truly exciting game.

Babe Ruth understood that reflexively, and he didn't give a damn if anyone disagreed.

As Bill James once pointed out, Christy Mathewson called his autobiography *Pitching in a Pinch* because back in the early 1900s, games only occasionally rose to the level of the "pinch," situations where contests could change dramatically. But when home runs abound, so does the possibility for immediate turnarounds. Home runs infuse baseball with talent, drama, hope.

They are proof that one man can make a difference.

A guy like Manny Ramirez drives traditionalists crazy. Ramirez could never have played for the old New York Giants of John McGraw, who advocated "scientific" small-ball for decades. Ramirez steps to the plate with one unwavering purpose in mind: to hit the hell out of the ball. He swings hard at every pitch. If a runner happens to advance while he's batting, it's a fortunate accident. He's an indifferent fielder and a controversial teammate.

As a result, fans and sportswriters often

criticize Ramirez for being selfish, just as, in days gone by, they knocked players as great as Ted Williams. Rarely does anyone stop to think that Ramirez may have consciously concluded that the best thing he can to do help his team win is to hit towering shots—or to think that such a conclusion is entirely reasonable.

And while the increasing rate of home runs after 1920 may well symbolize our nation's transition from an agrarian economy to an industrial powerhouse, as David Halberstam has written, it is also important to keep in mind that home runs are *fun*. Babe Ruth understood that, too.

It's in the spirit of enjoying the home run trot that this book aims to take you around the bases. *Dingers!* is organized into chronological chapters, but the last thing the world needs is another baseball book telling you that Dave Kingman led the National League in home runs in 1982, and then Mike Schmidt led in 1983, and then ...

Instead, each chapter contains a brief essay about the particular characteristics of an era in home run history and the era's premier home run hitter. A few themes run through all of these essays: the effects of ballparks, how rules and equipment changed, how homers related to other elements of the game. Then there are lists, charts, and graphs cataloging every kind of home run exploit that I could imagine, track down, and quantify.

For the most part, *Dingers!* encompasses events that took place in games of the National Association of Professional Baseball Leagues, which includes the U.S. major and minor leagues and the Mexican leagues, but not Japanese, Caribbean, amateur, or women's baseball. The latter were simply beyond the scope of what I could hope to research.

The one significant exception to this rule is the Negro Leagues, some of whose sluggers are profiled in Chapters 1 and 2. As with the other players on all the lists that follow, I hope I have been able to convey something about the time and place and the game they played, through the stories of their home runs.

One final list could contain all the home runs I wanted to fit into this book but wasn't able to.

Sorry, Chris Chambliss.

CHAPTER 1

1876-1919

Deadball

George Carlin used to perform a routine

about the differences between baseball and football. "Football has hitting, clipping, spearing, piling on, personal fouls, late hitting, and unnecessary roughness," he would say. "Baseball has the sacrifice." And then, "Football is played in any kind of weather: rain, snow, sleet, hail, fog. In baseball, if it rains, we don't go out to play."

HOME RUN BAKER

FIRST NATIONAL LEAGUE HOME RUN

SEVEN DAYS into the NL's first season in 1876, Chicago's Ross Barnes clouted the first round-tripper. Barnes sent the ball "straight down the left field to the carriages, for a clean home run" (according to a contemporary account) as the White Stockings beat the Cincinnati Reds, 15-9. Barnes, a second baseman and shortstop, won the league batting title that year with a .429 average. But he got on base with squibs, hitting balls hard into the ground so that they bounced once or twice, then rolled into foul territory—which counted as hits in 1876. After the rules were changed to count these "fair-foul hits" as foul balls, the batter who hit MLB's first home run quickly lost his effectiveness.

Carlin would go on

like this for a few minutes, barking descriptions of football and prancing his way through baseball phraseology, until he ended by observing that the core objectives of the two games are completely different.

Football: "With short bullet passes and long bombs, the quarterback marches his troops into enemy territory, balancing this aerial assault with a sustained ground attack that punches holes in the forward wall of the enemy's defensive line."

And baseball? "In baseball, the object is to go home! And to be safe! I hope I'll be safe at home!"

THEY CALLED THEM "HOME RUN"

THE ABILITY TO CRUSH home runs has given ballplayers some great nicknames, from The Sultan of Swat (Babe Ruth) to Beast (Jimmie Foxx) to Killer (Harmon Killebrew) to Hondo (Frank Howard) to Kong (Dave Kingman) to Big Papi (David Ortiz).

Funny thing, though: Almost all the men who have been called Home Run were deadball players, not sluggers. Back when nobody was hitting a lot of dingers, it only took a few to get tagged with the nickname Home Run.

Home Run Baker, of course, is the best example, with 96 career dingers in 13 seasons. But Charlie Duffee, who played from 1889 to 1893, was called Home Run although he hit only 35 taters in 508 career games. Neither Home Run Joe Marshall (1903, 1906) nor Charlie "Home Run" Johnson (six games in 1908) went deep even once in a major-league game.

Grant "Home Run" Johnson, a Negro Leagues star, may have been the best Home Run of them all. Johnson earned his nickname by reportedly hitting 60 homers for the Findlay Sluggers, a semipro team, in 1894. Johnson was decades ahead of his time: He studied pitchers the way Ted Williams would decades later, and his belief in clean living helped him play until he was 58 years old.

No. 1
HARRY DAVIS
67

No. 2
PIANO LEGS HICKMAN
58

No. 3
SAM CRAWFORD
57

No. 4
BUCK FREEMAN
54

No. 5T
SOCKS SEYBOLD
51

No. 5T
HONUS WAGNER
51

No. 7
NAP LAJOIE
47

No. 8
CY SEYMOUR
43

No. 9T
HOBE FERRIS
40

No. 9T
JIMMY WILLIAMS
40

MOST HOME RUNS

1900 1909

FIRST EXTRA-INNING HOME RUN

POP SNYDER, catcher for the Louisville Grays, hit the first extra-inning dinger in major-league history, a 10th-inning shot that helped beat the Boston Red Caps, 8-6, on June 29, 1876.

It was funny stuff, rooted in our understanding of the origins of our national pastimes. Baseball evolved from cricket before the Civil War, before America was an industrialized country. Indeed, the first game between two teams under rules that would be at least partially recognizable today took place in Hoboken, on a park overlooking the Hudson River, in 1845, when it was still possible to call a site in northern New Jersey the Elysian Fields without a trace of irony.

From the beginning, baseball's vocabulary had the pastoral tone that Carlin gently mocked. And so did its playbook. It's not that baseball as played was a clean game in the 19th century— as the sport evolved, it went through periods of widespread

PART I

DEATH *by* HOME RUN

- -

ALMOST COMPLETELY forgotten today, Jim Creighton was baseball's first superstar, first professional player— and first martyr.

Born in 1841, Creighton grew up in Brooklyn at a time when pitchers threw underhanded and stiff-armed, essentially tossing balls so that batters could put them into play. But Creighton figured out how to snap his wrist to get extra velocity—that is, how to throw a fastball. He eventually ended up with the Brooklyn Excelsiors.

Beginning in 1860, the Excelsiors toured the baseball-mad Northeast, dominating local opponents, with Creighton's hitting and pitching leading the way. On October 14, 1862, in the seventh inning of a game against the Morrisania Unions, Creighton smashed a pitch for a home run. But it cost him. In those days, hitters kept their hands apart on the bat, generating force by twisting their torso, and as Creighton delivered a mighty swing, the snapping sound was audible. Something inside his body had ruptured. Four days later, Creighton died. He was just 21.

violence, public drunkenness, and gambling.

But for the first 75 years of its history, baseball's tactics were those of a team sport that pitted baserunners against fielders as much as it did hitters against pitchers. All the various devices of batting selflessness that traditionalists prize today developed and came to dominate the game: bunting, taking pitches to allow stolen bases, moving runners over with ground balls, executing hit-and-run plays.

That's what happens when the home run is missing from baseball.

In baseball's earliest decades, players didn't think in terms of hitting for power, and neither did managers or executives. If a batter managed a four-base hit, fine, but attempting one seemed foolish. Henry Chadwick, one of the game's pioneers, once argued, "If the batsman hits the ball over the heads of the outfielders he gets his run at once, but at what cost? Why, at the expense of running 120 yards at his utmost speed...which involves an expenditure of muscular power needing a half-hour rest to recuperate from."

Even if players had tried to hit home runs, conditions were stacked against them. They couldn't swing for the fences, because there often weren't any fences at baseball's first fields. (The first concrete-and-steel stadium, Philadelphia's Shibe Park, didn't open until 1909.) More

MOST INSIDE-THE-PARK HOME RUNS, GAME

ON AUGUST 15, 1886, Guy Hecker hit three inside-the-park round-trippers to lead the Louisville Colonels of the American Association past the Baltimore Orioles, 22-5, in the second game of a doubleheader.

Splitting his time between the outfield, first base, and the mound, Hecker may have been the greatest hitting-pitching combo of the 19th century. He is still the only man ever to lead his league (the American Association) in batting average (.341, 1886) and wins (52, 1884). He also participated in the first major league players strike in 1889, when he and five teammates refused to play for Baltimore owner Mordecai Davidson, who liked to slap fines on players that were bigger than their paychecks.

On July 12, 1897, Tom McCreery of the NL Louisville Colonels tied Hecker's mark with three inside-the-park dingers, but nobody has matched it since. Dozens of players have had two in a game.

Probably the most surprising pair of insiders came on July 31, 1972, when White Sox first baseman Dick Allen, famous for hitting tape-measure shots, legged out two low-flying rockets against Minnesota that stayed within the confines of the Twins' Metropolitan Stadium.

important, they couldn't track pitches: Spitballs and scuffed balls were not only legal, but common, and balls discolored by tobacco juice, grass, and dirt routinely stayed in play.

The National League was launched in 1876 and spent the next 15 years adjusting its rules, usually to favor batters. For example, nine balls originally led to a walk; that number dropped to eight in 1880, seven in 1882, six in 1884, bobbed back to seven in 1886, and then went down to five in 1887, and finally four in 1889.

But fluctuations in scoring due to rules changes proved tem-

HOMERLESS WONDERS

IN 1877, the Chicago White Stockings (the NL club before they became the Cubs) hit zero home runs on their way to a 26–33 record. They are the only major league team to go without a dinger for an entire season.

EIGHT HOME RUNS IN ONE GAME?

ON JUNE 15, 1902, Corsicana beat Texarkana 51-3 in a Class D Texas League game, and—apparently—catcher Jay Justin "Nig" Clarke hit eight home runs.

Playing conditions that day were certainly conducive to big numbers. Sunday baseball was banned in Corsicana, so the game was moved to nearby Ennis, to a ballpark with bleachers running at a sharp angle across rightfield, whose foul pole may have been just 140 feet from home plate. Not only that, but Texarkana's pitcher was, according to Corsicana shortstop J. Walter Morris, toeing the slab, as a consequence of being the owner's son.

But it's still only "apparently" an eight-dinger day for Clarke, because contemporary accounts don't agree on the final score and the number of homers hit by Clarke and his teammates.

Tracked down by a *Sporting News* reporter in 1947, Clarke maintained he swatted the eight homers. True, he got his batting line wrong, as well as the opposing pitchers, the number of runs scored in the first three innings, and the reason the teams played in Ennis. But the National Association agrees with him: It recognizes Clarke's feat as the single-game minor-league home run record. So should we all.

four
Deadball
Home Runs
in one
GAME

THE LIST OF PLAYERS who hit four home runs in a game is filled with famed sluggers, Lou Gehrig, Chuck Klein, Gil Hodges, Willie Mays, and Mike Schmidt among them. But two deadball-era hitters paved the way: Hall of Famer Big Ed Delahanty, who owed much of his talent to genetics, and rail-thin second baseman Bobby Lowe, who owed it all to fish.

On Memorial Day, 1894, Lowe, playing for the Boston Beaneaters, went hitless in the first game of a doubleheader against the visiting Reds. Between games, he went to a local restaurant with his wife and stuffed himself to the gills with lobster, clams, and fish. He then proceeded to victimize Reds pitcher Icebox Chamberlin for four round-trippers in the second game, knocking two over the 250-foot leftfield fence in the third inning alone as Boston batted around. The Beaneaters eventually won, 20-11, and by the sixth inning, after Lowe's fourth dinger, their fans were so giddy they began tossing coins on the field in tribute. Lowe wound up collecting $160 that afternoon.

"The fish dinner did it," the superstitious Lowe told his teammates, and the next day he stuffed himself with seafood once more. But he failed to get a hit in a 22-8 loss against Cleveland.

Lowe never ate fish again.

On July 13, 1896, the Phillies' Delahanty equaled Lowe's feat with four taters off Chicago Colts pitcher Adonis Terry. Delahanty, the first Irish-American superstar, had the game in his blood—four of his seven brothers played in the majors—and over the course of his career, the strapping 190-pounder hit .400 three times and won batting titles in both leagues on the way to compiling a lifetime .346 average.

But his entry into the four-dinger club took a bit more effort than Lowe's. Two of Delahanty's four shots at Chicago's tough West Side Grounds, where centerfield was 560 feet away from home plate, were inside-the-park jobs, and Big Ed had to leg it around the bases in a hurry. His other two blasts cleared the park's 35-foot fence.

Unfortunately, the hard-drinking Delahanty wasn't much for discipline. In June, 1903, Washington suspended him for excessive boozing. Leaving the Senators in Detroit, he caught a train back to New York and got thrown off near Niagara Falls, either for being drunk and disorderly, fighting with the conductor, or both. Walking along the tracks, he somehow plunged off the International Bridge, into the river below. Did he fall? Did he jump? Was he pushed? 103 years later, it's still not clear.

FIRST PINCH-
HIT HOME RUN

IT TOOK 16 YEARS after
the launch of the National
League for a pinch-hitter
to homer in the big
leagues. Tom Daly did it
on May 14, 1892, but the
Boston Beaneaters beat
his Brooklyn Bridegrooms,
8-7—and yes, that's
really what the teams
were called back then.

porary, as pitchers kept discovering ways to assert their advan-
tages. Even when the pitching mound was moved back from 50
feet to its modern distance of 60 feet 6 inches from home plate
in 1893, the boost to batters didn't last. National League scoring
dropped from 7.36 runs per team per game in 1894 to 4.96 in
1898 to 3.98 in 1902 to 3.57 in 1906. That year, the White Sox,
who had a team OPS under .600 and were called the Hitless
Wonders, beat the Cubs in six games to win the World Series

Popular culture celebrated small ball in the 19th century.
The first baseball hit song was "Slide, Kelly, Slide," which fans
sang to Boston Beaneaters outfielder Mike "King" Kelly in
1889: "Your running's a disgrace! Stay there, hold your base!"

New statistics did, too. That same year, *The New York Times*
wrote that it would start including sacrifices in boxscores
"with a view of promoting more team work among players."

Among the flotilla of players who did manage to hit more than
a handful of home runs before 1920, two are worth remembering
for reasons beyond those history has attached to their names.

Ned Williamson, also known as Ed. (complete with a period),
set the single-season home run record (27) that Babe Ruth broke
in 1919 with 29. If Williamson is remembered at all today, it's for
the utterly fluky nature of that mark: He hit those 27 homers in
1884, but never had more than nine in any other season.

The season before setting his then-astonishing record, Williamson hit 49 doubles, then an NL record, at Chicago's Lake
Front Park, where balls that flew over the short rightfield fence,
just 196 feet from home plate, counted as two-base hits. But
before the 1884 season, the ground rules were changed to count
fly balls over the short porch as home runs—and Williamson proceeded to crack 25 dingers at home and just two on the road.

As a team, Chicago hit 131 home runs at Lake Front Park and 11 away from home—one of baseball's truly unbreakable records (the club moved the following season).

There was, however, more to Williamson than the craziness of 1884. In an 1894 survey by the *Reach Guide* of a dozen prominent baseball old-timers, Williamson got more votes than anyone else as the best player of all time. In 1900, future Hall of Famer Cap Anson, who played pro ball for 27 years, called Williamson "the greatest all-around ballplayer the country ever saw."

The praise stemmed, in part, from Williamson's amazing fielding. Playing at a time when defense was much more important than it is today, Williamson, a third baseman and shortstop, led the league at his position in assists seven times, double plays six times, and fielding average four times.

MOST HOME RUNS ALLOWED IN ONE GAME

ON JUNE 12, 1886, Charlie Sweeney, pitching for the St. Louis Maroons in the National League, surrendered seven dingers to the Detroit Wolverines, the most ever in one game. (Amazingly, he gave up only nine dingers the whole season.)

Sweeney had a brief, wild career. At the age of 21, he was the hardest thrower in baseball. On June 7, 1884, Sweeney struck out 19 batters for the Providence Grays in a nine-inning game against Boston, setting a record that was tied four times but went unbroken for 102 years. (He also batted cleanup that day.) He had 17 wins by July 22, when he managed to get himself thrown off the Grays after an altercation with manager Frank Bancroft.

Starting a game against Philadelphia, Sweeney was hung over and possibly still drinking. He refused to come out of the game and was finally ordered off the mound in the middle of the contest. He jumped to the St. Louis Maroons, then in the Union Association, where he went 24–7—in that same 1894 season.

His career went sharply downhill after that. In 1885, he was 11–21, in 1886 he was 5–6, and he ended his career going 0–3 for Cleveland in the American Association. He was 24.

In 1894, Sweeney killed a man in a San Francisco saloon. He umpired a California League game in 1898 after serving time for manslaughter at San Quentin, beginning that penitentiary's long association with sports.

Between 1888 and 1940, 10 pitchers allowed six homers in a game. After that, it certainly looked as if modern bullpens would never again allow a starter to absorb such a shellacking. Then, on August 8, 2004, Tim Wakefield of the Red Sox gave up six homers in five innings at Detroit—and won the game. Boston beat the Tigers, 11-9.

Williamson supported black players' attempts to play in the major leagues in the 1880s, noting that "haughty Caucasians say it's okay to have darkies carry water, but not in the lineup." He was also one of the first to join the players union, called the National Brotherhood of Base Ball Players, that started in 1885.

On March 8, 1889, in an exhibition game in Paris, Williamson tore up his knee on a gravelly field near the Eiffel Tower. A local doctor botched his treatment, and, literally adding insult to injury, team owner Albert Spald-ing refused to pay Williamson's medical bill. Williamson tried playing again for the White Stockings in 1889 and for the Chicago Pirates of the Players League the following season, but his performance collapsed. So did the Players League, and soon after that, the Brotherhood.

Williamson then opened a saloon, a disastrous decision seeing as he already drank too much. Suffering from kidney failure and ballooned to nearly 300 pounds, he died in 1894 at the age of 36. Today he lies in an unmarked grave in Chicago's Rosehill Cemetery.

THE NEW YORK, New Haven, and Hartford Railroad ran along the third-base side of Boston's South End Grounds, where the Beaneaters used to play before they were renamed the Braves. Beyond the outfield there was a roundhouse, a circular building for storing and switching trains.

Tradition has it that Chief Zimmer, an outstanding defensive catcher in the 1890s, once knocked a home run out of the park and onto a coal car headed for Albany. The ball was allegedly retrieved when the train stopped in Fall River, Massachusetts.

For more than 100 years, baseball reference books have cited the "200-Mile Home Run" without challenge, and it's one of the enduring legends of baseball lore. Even Bill James, in his *Historical Baseball Abstract*, cities the "200-Mile Homer" as one of the two things for which Zimmer was most famous. (The other: "Zimmer's Base Ball Game," which came out in 1893. It was cited as "one most beautiful baseball table games ever created" by *The National Pastime*, published in 1984.)

Did it really happen?

Sure it did.

Never mind that Albany's about 170 miles west of Boston and Fall River's about 50 miles south.

Some things are just true.

"Just one [superstition]: Whenever I hit a home run, I make certain I touch all four bases."

-Babe Ruth

FIRST AMERICAN LEAGUE HOME RUN

ON OPENING DAY, 1901, Cleveland Blues second baseman Erve Beck hit the American League's first extra-base hit, a double. The next day, April 25, he cracked the AL's first homer. The dinger came in a losing cause, as the White Sox beat the Blues, 7-3.

Frank "Home Run" Baker is known for how few home runs he hit, despite his nickname: His career high was 12, in 1913. But that's misleading.

Baker, who grew up on a farm in Trappe, Maryland, was the third baseman in the "$100,000 infield" of Connie Mack's Philadelphia A's, along with first baseman Stuffy McInnis, second baseman Eddie Collins, and shortstop Jack Barry. Those clubs won four pennants and three World Series, with Baker contributing impressive power for that era. He led the AL in home runs for four straight years from 1911 through 1914. He also topped the league in RBI by a margin of 21 in 1912 and 27 in 1913.

Baker fully earned his nickname in the 1911 World Series, a dramatic affair on and off the field. After John McGraw's Giants won the first game, Game 2 was tied, 1-1, with two out in the sixth inning when Baker came to bat against Rube Marquard. Eddie Collins, the runner on second, noticed Marquard

BALLPARKS WITH MOST HOME RUNS

11,200 WRIGLEY FIELD	Chicago 1914–	
11,113 TIGER STADIUM	Detroit 1912–1999	
10,726 YANKEE STADIUM	New York 1923–1973 1976–	
10,413 FENWAY PARK	Boston 1912–	
8,268 SPORTSMAN'S PARK	St. Louis 1902–1966	
6,965 SHIBE PARK	Philadelphia 1909–1970	
6,659 MUNICIPAL STADIUM	Cleveland 1932–1993	
6,658 POLO GROUNDS	New York 1910–1963	
6,250 COMISKEY PARK	Chicago 1910–1990	
5,828 COUNTY STADIUM	Milwaukee 1953–1965 1970–2000	

flash a fastball signal, and Collins in turn passed a signal to Baker, who cracked the pitch over the rightfield fence at Shibe Park in Philadelphia.

Christy Mathewson's (ghostwritten) newspaper column the next day ripped Marquard, but Matty didn't fare any better in Game 3 at the Polo Grounds. Two outs away from completing a 1-0 shutout, Mathewson delivered a 2-1 curveball to Baker, who lined another home run to rightfield. The crowd fell so silent that Baker's footsteps could be heard as he trotted the bases. The A's won the contest in the 11th inning and the Series in six games, and Baker was forever after "Home Run."

Wrote one poet from his home state of Maryland:

"Somewhere little glooms abide
While busy spellers hawk,
But they never speak of Baker's name
In little old New Yawk."

In 1911, Baker beat out Ty Cobb by three dingers for the AL home run title, 11–8, depriving Cobb of a Triple Crown. In 1914, Walter Johnson, whom Baker tagged for five career homers, threw the only reported beanball of his career, aiming a fastball at (but missing) Baker's head. Baker played in six World Series, batting .363 with 18 RBI in 25 games.

MOST INSIDE-THE-PARK HOME RUNS, *Season*

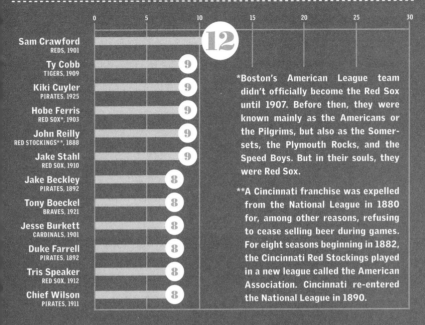

Sam Crawford	REDS, 1901	12
Ty Cobb	TIGERS, 1909	9
Kiki Cuyler	PIRATES, 1925	9
Hobe Ferris	RED SOX*, 1903	9
John Reilly	RED STOCKINGS**, 1888	9
Jake Stahl	RED SOX, 1910	9
Jake Beckley	PIRATES, 1892	8
Tony Boeckel	BRAVES, 1921	8
Jesse Burkett	CARDINALS, 1901	8
Duke Farrell	PIRATES, 1892	8
Tris Speaker	RED SOX, 1912	8
Chief Wilson	PIRATES, 1911	8

*Boston's American League team didn't officially become the Red Sox until 1907. Before then, they were known mainly as the Americans or the Pilgrims, but also as the Somersets, the Plymouth Rocks, and the Speed Boys. But in their souls, they were Red Sox.

**A Cincinnati franchise was expelled from the National League in 1880 for, among other reasons, refusing to cease selling beer during games. For eight seasons beginning in 1882, the Cincinnati Red Stockings played in a new league called the American Association. Cincinnati re-entered the National League in 1890.

MOST INSIDE-THE-PARK HOME RUNS, *Career*

Jesse Burkett	55
Sam Crawford	52
Tommy Leach	49
Ty Cobb	48
Honus Wagner	43
Tris Speaker	40
Jake Beckley	38
Rogers Hornsby	33
Edd Roush	31
Jake Daubert	30
Willie Keeler	30

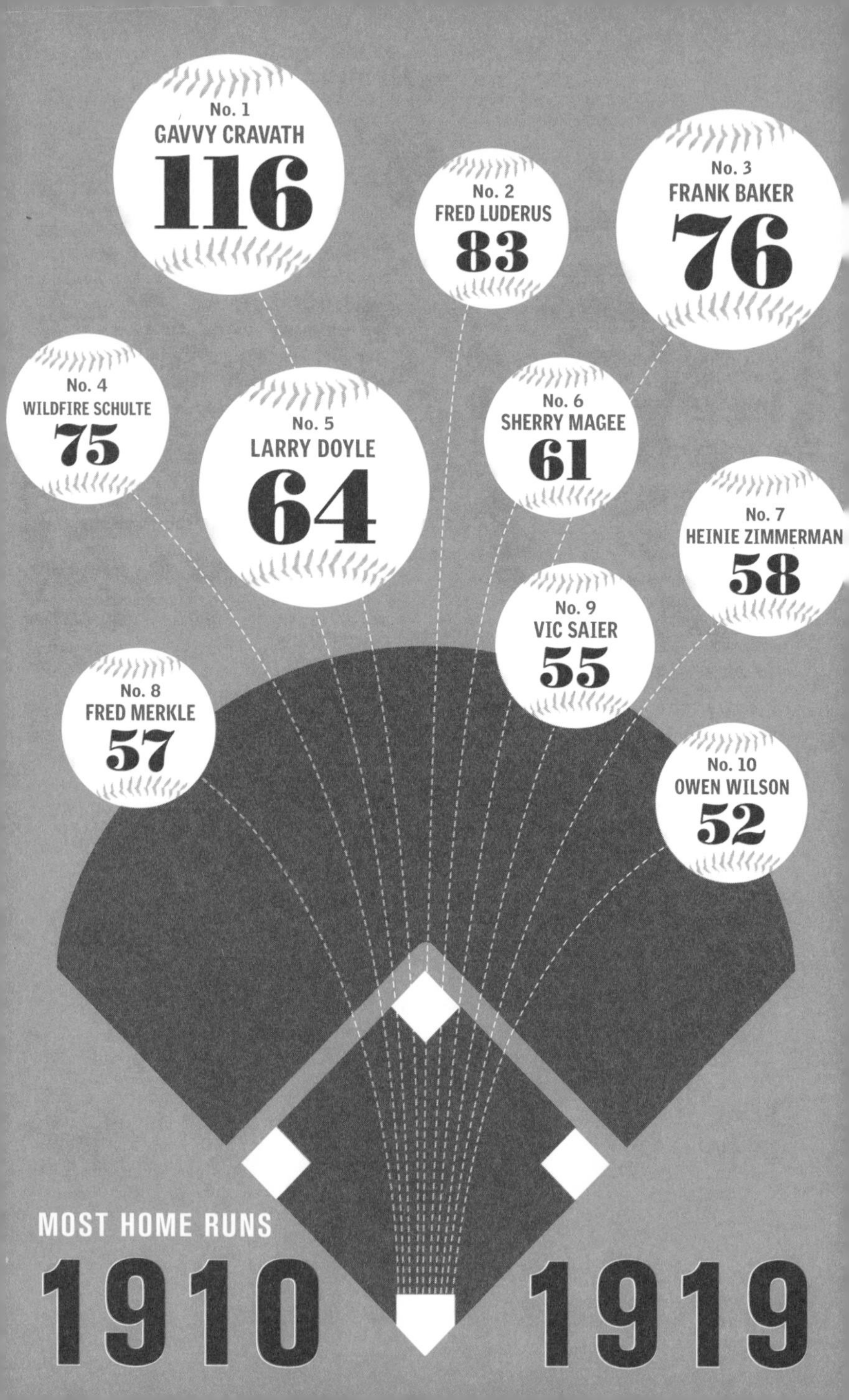

No. 1
GAVVY CRAVATH
116

No. 2
FRED LUDERUS
83

No. 3
FRANK BAKER
76

No. 4
WILDFIRE SCHULTE
75

No. 5
LARRY DOYLE
64

No. 6
SHERRY MAGEE
61

No. 7
HEINIE ZIMMERMAN
58

No. 8
FRED MERKLE
57

No. 9
VIC SAIER
55

No. 10
OWEN WILSON
52

MOST HOME RUNS

1910   1919

Baker left the major leagues twice, once in 1915 over a salary dispute and again in 1920, when his wife and daughter contracted scarlet fever (his wife terminally). Each time he returned after a year off to play for the Yankees—effectively from 1916 to 1919 and less so from 1921 to 1922. As a manager in Maryland's Eastern Shore League in 1924, he discovered 16-year-old Jimmie Foxx and sold his rights to Mack for just $2,000.

Add up Baker's career numbers and look at them in the context of his era, and you can make a good case for him being the greatest third baseman in baseball history before Eddie Mathews (and then Mike Schmidt and George Brett). Yet Baker inexplicably had to wait until 1955 to make it into the Hall of Fame.

But as Home Run Baker himself remarked, "It's better to get a rosebud while you're alive than a whole bouquet after you're dead."

The greatest team of the Deadball Era was the 1906–1910 Chicago Cubs, who went

SAY IT AIN'T SO
(Okay, It Ain't.)

AND THEN THERE'S the legendary homer hit in the early 1900s by Andy Oyler, a 140-pound third baseman, for the Minneapolis Millers of the American Association. This dinger came in a game the Millers played against the St. Paul Apostles (later the Saints) one rainy day in Minneapolis shortly after the playing field had been turned into a giant mud pie by a touring circus.

The story goes that Oyler turned to avoid getting beaned by a pitch, whereupon the ball hit his bat—and disappeared. As Oyler ran the bases, Apostles players yelled that he had the ball in his pockets, but Oyler yelled back, "I ain't got it!" He scooted all the way around to home plate before the ball was found, only a couple of feet from home plate, in a muddy tent-pole hole the circus had left behind.

The account of this feat was repeated as gospel over the years by descendants of Oyler's teammates, and retold in books, magazines, and baseball histories, not to mention by the great Hall-of-Fame broadcaster Ernie Harwell. A ball that traveled only a few feet somehow rolled, over the decades, from undocumented curiosity all the way to accepted fact.

Ah … hold on. It never happened. That's what Oyler himself told a reporter in 1955, 15 years before his death. He took particular exception to the claim that he used the word the word "ain't."

"I didn't finish college," said Oyler, "but I was never guilty of anything like that."

530–235 (a .693 clip) in those five years. In 1906, when they won a record 116 games, the Cubs allowed just 1,018 hits all season, only 12 of which were home runs.

Yet despite the Cubs' dominance, statheads routinely deride Cooperstown's enshrinement of first baseman Frank Chance, second baseman Johnny Evers, and shortstop Joe Tinker, who entered the Hall of Fame together in 1946. Now, that's silly. Any team good enough

to dominate its league for more than a couple of seasons will usually have three or four (or more) Hall of Famers, and Three Finger Brown wasn't dragging Chicago to the pennant every year by himself.

But it's true that if you look at the numbers the Cubs lineup put up, even if you try to adjust them for the fact that they played when runs were scarce, they don't seem all that special. The reality is that the Cubs were

from
The New York American
June 15, 1915

CONTEMPORARY COVERAGE

Autobiography of a Home Run by Itself

in Collaboration with Damon Runyon

BEFORE DAMON RUNYON wrote short stories such as "All Horse Players Die Broke" and Broadway plays such as *Guys and Dolls*, he covered baseball for the *American*, part of Hearst newspaper chain. He did so with the eye for unusual characters and skeptical good humor that he also brought to his later, more famous work. When a ballgame itself didn't hold his interest, he wrote about it from the perspective of anyone nearby, from gamblers to groundskeepers.

Or, in the case of a 1915 doubleheader between two dreary teams, a home run.

I AM a Home Run.

If I wanted to be right chesty about it, I might tell you that I am THE Home Run, and you would never know any better, but I am an honest Home Run, and as modest and unassuming as Ed Sweeney's batting average.

Besides that, there are some Home Runs that I wouldn't want to be for the price of two week's board and room at Long Beach; disreputable and characterless Home Runs

incredible at the "things that don't show up in boxscores" and that today's announcers like to extol, such as preventing baserunners through great defense.

A century later, what's most different about today's game is the regular presence of home runs. The home run tilted the game back to hitters and made the confrontation between pitcher and batter its central drama. It tightly bound team success to individual acts, such as going yard and driving in runs—acts that do show up in boxscores.

Frankly, the home run also made the game more vulgar. But by 1918, a year in which a guy named Charlie Hollocher led the National League with 161 hits and nobody hit more than 11 homers, a little vulgarity is what baseball desperately needed.

And so, on cue, up to the plate stepped George Herman Ruth.

that are always running around in loose box scores, never caring who hits 'em, and bringing odium upon a good old family name ...

Anytime you see a Home Run letting pitchers hit 'em, you can wager there is something wrong somewhere. I do not even except these Home Runs that are being hit by this [Yankees pitcher] Ray Caldwell, although we are giving them the benefit of the doubt until we make a thorough investigation. They are either spurious, or this Caldwell is an outfielder at heart, and not a pitcher at all ...

If you will pick up your favorite newspaper this morning you will find that I figured prominently in the doubleheader that was played at the Polo Grounds yesterday afternoon by the Yankees and the St. Louis Browns ... The score of the first game was 12 to 7, and the count in the second pastime was 5 to 4 in 10 innings. I was largely responsible for many of those tallies, just as your paper states if it tells the truth about me and five other Home Runs ...

Now then, before I go any further, I suppose you would like to learn a little about my history. Well, I was born in Section 1, of Rule 48, of the Official Playing Rules, and I have been around a long time. My habitat is the left-field bleachers, the right-field stand, or the remote corners of the baseball yard, and I am often indigenous to the pitching of Grover Lowdermilk, Harry Hoch, Ray Keating, Lefty Weilman and even Ray Fisher. If you want to get me when I [get] right good, however, drop in when Rube Marquard has left the hop on his fast one in his apartment. I can bounce mighty far off a hickory stick these days, I tell you what ...

I was not Clarence Walker's second circuit clout into the leftfield bleachers in the ninth inning of the second game with a runner aboard, although I don't mind saying that I am a full brother to that Home Run, and taught it all it knows ... [Yankees manager] Wild William Donovan sent up Birdie Cree to bat for Walter Pipp, and I don't mind confiding in you here and now that I was lurking in the background ready to do my duty for Birdie had I been needed. I would have been that Home Run that Birdie would have busted had I been called upon, but he used one of those weakling singles to the right-field wall, and the game was over.

BABE RUTH

CHAPTER 2

1920-1945

The Rise of Power

In early 1920, a reporter for *The Sporting News* named Fred Lieb made a proposal to baseball's Rules Committee, on which he served as a non-voting member. Until that time, if a hit immediately ended a game, only the winning run would count, even in the case of what would today be called a walkoff home run.

THE RAJAH

ROGERS HORNSBY is the only player with more than 300 dingers to hit 30 or more inside-the-park home runs. Of Rajah's 301 career homers, 33 stayed within stadium walls. Hornsby was also the first batter to pinch-hit a walkoff grand slam, coming off the bench for the Cubs to clear the bases in the bottom of the 11th inning against the Braves on September 13, 1931.

Suppose a contest was tied,

2-2, in the bottom of the 13th inning with men on first and second and you knocked a dinger out of the park. The game would have ended with a score of 3-2 and you would have been credited with a double and one run batted in. Lieb suggested counting these home runs as home runs, just as they would be scored if they were hit in other innings.

Lieb's proposal passed by a vote of 5 to 1, but umpire Hank O'Day, one of the National League's representatives on the committee, objected vehemently. O'Day beat his fist on the table and yelled, "I'm telling you, it is illegal. You can't score runs after a game is over!"

And of course, O'Day was right. You can't score runs after

MOST HOME RUNS WITH MEN ON BASE

ONLY EIGHT PLAYERS have hit 30 or more home runs in a season with men on base. Babe Ruth and Mark McGwire did it twice.

		HR with men on base	HR, season total
Babe Ruth, Yankees	1921	37	59
Mark McGwire, Cardinals	1998	37	70
Hack Wilson, Cubs	1930	33	56
Manny Ramirez, Red Sox	2005	32	45
Babe Ruth, Yankees	1927	30	60
Jim Gentile, Orioles	1961	30	46
Harmon Killebrew, Twins	1962	30	48
Hank Aaron, Braves	1970	30	38
Mark McGwire, Cardinals	1999	30	65
Luis Gonzalez, Diamondbacks	2001	30	57

No. 1
BABE RUTH
467

No. 2
ROGERS HORNSBY
250

No. 3
CY WILLIAMS
202

No. 4
KEN WILLIAMS
190

No. 5T
JIM BOTTOMLEY
146

No. 5T
LOU GEHRIG
146

No. 7
BOB MEUSEL
146

No. 8
HARRY HEILMANN
142

No. 9
HACK WILSON
137

No. 10
GEORGE KELLY
134

MOST HOME RUNS
1920 1929

MOST HOME RUNS IN ONE *Ballpark* BY A VISITING PLAYER, SEASON

1. Harry Heilmann, TIGERS — **10**
1922 Shibe Park, Philadelphia

2T. Lou Gehrig, YANKEES — **9**
1931 Sportsman's Park, St. Louis

2T. Jimmie Foxx, ATHLETICS — **9**
1932 Tiger Stadium, Detroit

2T. Stan Spence, SENATORS — **9**
1943 Sportsman's Park, St. Louis

2T. Joe Adcock, BRAVES — **9**
1954 Ebbets Field, Brooklyn

2T. Willie Mays, GIANTS — **9**
1954 Ebbets Field, Brooklyn

HARRY HEILMANN IS famous for his batting prowess in odd-numbered years: He won batting titles in 1921, 1923 (when he hit .403), 1925, and 1927. The Hall of Fame Tigers outfielder also figures in one of the best stories about the contrasting styles great hitters can have. When Ted Williams was chasing .400 in the late days of the 1941 season, he sought out the retired Heilmann, who had been the last AL hitter to pass that mark, and asked his advice. When George Brett was pursuing .400 in 1980 and was told that his batting stats were similar to the numbers Heilmann put up in 1923, Brett replied, "Who the hell is Harry Heilmann?"

Heilmann arrived in the big leagues in 1914 at the age of 19. A teammate of Ty Cobb and a good hitter for several seasons, he was one of the players most helped by the changes in baseball that started in 1920. In 1921, his OPS rocketed from .787 to 1.051, and never dropped below .897 until his final season.

Curiously, though, the 21 home runs Heilmann hit in 1922 were a career high, and it's a surprise to see him rather than, say, Joe Adcock—a massive power hitter who murdered the Dodgers—at the top of this list.

Shibe Park is the key. The Philadelphia stadium had already boosted home run totals in previous seasons, but in 1922, the Athletics brought the fences in by 46 feet in left-field and 34 feet in center. The A's, who had allowed 59 dingers at home the previous year, surrendered 82, the most in baseball (while giving up just 25 on the road), so obviously Heilmann was among the right-handed hitters who adjusted before the pitchers did.

Despite his relatively modest home run output—he averaged just under 11 dingers a year in 17 big-league seasons—Heilmann, with a lifetime .342 BA, had a muscular nickname: Slug.

a game is over. Unless, of course, you hit a home run.

With that rule change, baseball made official an idea that would only grow stronger with time: that the act of hitting a home run was more important than the logic of the game.

By 1920, conditions for a power surge had been brewing for a couple of seasons. Through the 1910s, attendance had drooped, along with run production (the 235 home runs hit in the majors in 1918 were the lowest total ever), but both had soared in 1919, as erstwhile pitcher Babe Ruth slammed a then-record 29 homers with an AL-leading 114 RBI for the Red Sox.

★ HOME RUN RELICS ★

THE NATIONAL BASEBALL HALL OF FAME opened on June 12, 1939, and today averages about 350,000 visitors a year. The Hall is studded with exhibits showcasing home runs and the men who hit them, drawn from a collection that includes 1,796 bats (203 are associated with home runs) and 6,490 baseballs (81 related to home runs).

While there's really no substitute for visiting Cooperstown, one ongoing online "exhibit" features the stories of the seven players who have held the single-season home run record. Working backward, you've probably heard of Barry Bonds, Mark McGwire, Roger Maris, and Babe Ruth, and maybe Ned Williamson, but what about the next three guys: Harry Stovey, Charley Jones, and George Hall?

Another online exhibit offers a tribute to the "Shot Heard 'Round the World," where you can listen to Russ Hodges' famous radio call of Bobby Thomson's 1951 pennant-clinching home run.

So even if you can't go to Cooperstown today, you can go online to the Hall at baseballhalloffame.org.

Then it was revealed that a group of White Sox players had conspired with gamblers to throw the 1919 World Series. When that scandal broke, it petrified baseball's owners. Within a year, they had vested substantial power in a new commissioner's office and instructed the first Commissioner of Baseball, a former federal district judge in Illinois named Kenesaw Mountain Landis, to go after the cheats.

So if Ruth represented some strange new development in the game, the owners not only weren't inclined to block him, they weren't in a good position to try.

Baseball also imposed a limited ban on the spitball in the winter of 1919–20. Players had complained that

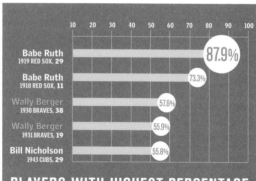

PLAYERS WITH HIGHEST PERCENTAGE OF TEAM HOME RUNS (Minimum 10 HR by player)

PLAYING SEVEN-PLUS years for Boston, Wally Berger smacked 103 homers out of Braves Field, where winds often blew straight in from centerfield to make the cavernous dimensions even crueler. In 1930, Berger clocked 38 HRs in a one-man-show rookie season. The next highest total on the team belonged to Buster Chatham, who hit all of five.

IF HE DIDN'T HAVE BAD LUCK...

TWO BASEBALLS famously flew out of Chicago's old Comiskey Park. Babe Ruth clouted the first, over the grandstand rooftop in right, in 1927. Fifteen newspaper writers from New York, Chicago, and elsewhere were on hand to marvel in print at the blast. The second, swatted in 1936, flew the other way, over the leftfield roof, and to far fewer accolades.

It was clubbed by The Beast, Jimmie Foxx.

Foxx, one of the game's most ferocious sluggers, was so strong that other players used to say "even his sweat has muscles." A three-time MVP, he won the Triple Crown in 1933. His 534 career round-trippers, many of them tape-measure shots, in 20 seasons with the A's and Red Sox put him second behind Ruth when he quit.

Yet Double X doesn't often come to mind when fans discuss the game's immortals, largely because he had terrible luck. Foxx had the misfortune to compete directly against Ruth, the greatest slugger of all time, and Lou Gehrig, the greatest first baseman ever. Chasing Ruth during his stellar 1932 season, Foxx lost two homers when games were rained out before they became

official. And a wire screen atop Sportsman's Park's rightfield wall—a screen that hadn't been in place when Ruth set the home run record in 1927—turned at least three more would-be homers into doubles. Sixty dingers were all Foxx needed for immortality. He wound up with 58.

The fastball-loving, hard-drinking Foxx left baseball two years too early to qualify for the league's pension plan. And he lost what little he had earned playing during his prime for the cash-strapped A's to bad investments and more bad luck. He ended his days working for the Bureau for Unemployment Compensation for just $4,000 a year. Foxx's hard living caught up to him fast, and health troubles plagued him: heart attacks, high blood pressure, hernias, head injuries.

None of this was lost on the taciturn Foxx. "I've been on the wrong side of everything," the 52-year-old slugger said in 1960, a year before he was forced into bankruptcy. "I've had nothing but bad luck since I got out of baseball."

Seven years later, he left the park for good. Cause of death: choking on a piece of meat.

discolored balls were hard to control and to see. Besides that, an influenza pandemic had spread around the world in 1918 and 1919, which raised concerns that spitballs might be as infectious as they were unsanitary. Then, on August 16, 1920, the Indians' Ray Chapman became the only modern major-league player to be killed by a pitch when the Yankees' Carl Mays hit him in the temple.

The following winter, spitballs and scuffed balls were banned outright, and teams started keeping fresh balls available for play. The improved visibility of balls—and not any radical change in their liveliness—was a mighty help to hitters.

And then there was Ruth himself.

One thing to appreciate about the Babe is that by 1920, he was already the most legendary home run hitter in the game. Even when he was toiling as a starting pitcher for Boston, his effortlessly prodigious blasts attracted huge attention. Ruth hit only four dingers in 1915, for example, but two of them went into the upper stands at the Polo Grounds and

MOST TIMES HIT
FOR THE CYCLE

TWO PLAYERS HAVE HIT for the cycle more than any others: 1920s Yankee Bob Meusel and 1920s Dodger Babe Herman, each three times.

In viewing "similarity scores" devised by Bill James—a formula that compares players' raw stats across a series of offensive categories and adjusts the result for position—the player Meusel is most comparable to is ... Herman.

For his career, Meusel hit .309 with 156 homers and 1,067 runs batted in; Herman batted .324 with 181 dingers and 997 RBI. That's not completely surprising. Both men had, after all, what it takes to hit for the cycle: power, speed, and the ability to hit for average.

But there the similarities end. Meusel, an outfielder with a rocket arm and a great glove, was the no. 5 hitter, behind Babe Ruth and Lou Gehrig, in the lineup of Murderers' Row. But he was surly and unpopular, and was gone from the game after 11 seasons. Yankees manager Miller Huggins said Meusel was too indifferent to get the most out of his talent, and maybe he was right.

Herman was as clumsy a fielder as Meusel was slick and as lovable as Meusel was unpleasant. He led the NL in errors at two different positions in consecutive seasons (first base in 1927, outfield in 1928), but was a hugely popular player.

A member of the Brooklyn club whose bumbling players and front office earned them the nickname the Daffiness Boys,

another landed in the rightfield bleachers at Fenway Park. His final shot of the year left Sportsman's Park in St. Louis and broke a window in a building across the street.

In 1916, Ruth hit just three homers, but they came in three consecutive games, which stirred up a buzz. "The more I see of Babe, the more he seems a figure out of mythology," one writer gushed in 1918. By then, Ruth was raring to play full time, and his determination to mash as many taters as possible was only stoked further when the Red Sox sold him to

the Yankees before the 1920 season.

Ruth held his bat at the end, without choking up, and swung hard, all the time focusing on his follow-through. "The harder you grip the bat, the more you can swing it through the ball and the farther the ball will go," he said. "I swing big, with everything I've got. I hit big or miss big. I like to live as big as I can."

Deadball proponents were appalled by that philosophy. Watching Ruth hit a shot over a group of palm trees during spring training in 1919, Giants manager John McGraw, the lead-

Herman was famed for "doubling into a double play" against the Braves in 1926. On August 15, with the bases loaded, Herman smashed a ball off the rightfield wall at Ebbets Field. Dazzy Vance, the runner on second, rounded third base for home but then turned back. Chick Fewster, the runner on first, stopped at third. But Herman, heading for a triple, slid into third, too. Herman was called out for passing Fewster, and Fewster, who wasn't out yet, was tagged when he mistakenly began walking off the field with Babe.

For years afterward, the team had to live down the joke:

"The Dodgers have three men on base."

"Yeah? Which base?"

In 1930, Herman hit .393 and posted an OPS of 1.132. His batting average, hits (241), extra-base hits (94), total bases (416), slugging percentage (.678), and on-base percentage (.455) are all Dodgers records. The entire National League hit .303 that year, so there's a lot of air to let out of those numbers, but it was a legitimately outstanding season.

The lesser Babe made the season even more memorable when he was passed by a hitter running the bases, nullifying what should have been a home run—twice.

After leaving the big leagues in 1937, Herman played in the minors. The Dodgers brought him home in 1945, signing him to their wartime roster. In his first at-bat upon his return, Herman smacked a single—and stumbled over first base.

FIRST HOME RUN AFTER DARK

BABE HERMAN hit the first home run in a night game on July 10, 1935, in Cincinnati. Herman's Reds beat the Dodgers, 15-2.

ing advocate of so-called "scientific baseball," said, "If he plays every day, the bum will hit into 100 double plays before the season is over."

Ty Cobb, who fully understood the threat Ruth represented to his style of play, called the Babe "nigger" and asked people if they smelled anything when Ruth was around.

Ruth didn't care. Like American achievers from James Madison to Charles Lindbergh to LeBron James, he didn't wait around for anyone to tell him what to do; he invented his own path to greatness. And if the greatest manager and the greatest player of the day objected, they could go to hell while the Babe set records and won pennants.

So the stage was set for the revolution of 1920. An already confident superstar was moving from an unfriendly park (Ruth

Babe Ruth's
"called shot"
1932

Ted Williams'
home run
in his final at-bat
1960

George Brett's
pine-tar home run
1983

Carlos Martinez'
home run off Jose
Canseco's head
1993

Fernando Tatis'
second grand slam
in one inning
1999

GREATEST NOVELTY HOME RUNS as voted by ESPN.com readers

OCTOBER 2, 2003, was the 25th anniversary of Bucky Dent's historic dinger over the Green Monster at Fenway Park. To celebrate that anniversary, ESPN.com published its list of the 100 greatest homers of all time—Bill Mazeroski's 1960

World Series winner ranked no. 1—and asked readers to choose the greatest novelty dinger from its compilation. Even 71 years after the fact—or, rather, fiction—Ruth's most mythical blast was tops with fans.

the
BLACK BABE RUTH

NEGRO LEAGUES CATCHER Josh Gibson was the "black Babe Ruth," a man who hit so many home runs so far that he became the standard of comparison for teammates and rivals. His most renowned shot came in 1930, when legend has it that the 18-year-old rookie hit a ball out of Yankee Stadium.

The House that Ruth Built opened its doors to black teams for the first time that season, and Gibson's Pittsburgh-based Homestead Grays had come to the Bronx as part of a nine-game playoff against the New York Lincoln Giants.

In the second game of the series in Pittsburgh, Gibson became the first batter to send a ball over the left-centerfield wall at Forbes Field, which, at 457 feet from home plate, was the deepest part of the park. (Only four players matched that feat afterward: Oscar Charleston—Gibson's teammate—Mickey Mantle, Dick Stuart, and Gibson himself in 1946.)

During the sixth game, at Yankee Stadium on September 27, Broadway Connie Rector of the Giants served Gibson a changeup. The barrel-chested Gibson crushed it, roping the ball so deep to left- field that many people believed it left the stadium. Orlando Cepeda, whose father played with Gibson in Puerto Rico, once said, "I heard it bounced off the subway train."

In fact, Gibson probably just missed becoming the only player to hit a fair ball out of Yankee Stadium. John Holway, the dean of Negro Leagues researchers, who interviewed the game's surviving participants decades later, concluded that Gibson's ball slammed against the top of the back wall of the bullpen, located between the grandstand and bleachers in leftfield. "Another two feet and it would have cleared the stadium altogether."

Gibson's Hall of Fame plaque says he hit "almost 800" home runs in his 17-year career, which conflates statistics from games played under all kinds of conditions. And even after all the research of recent years, it can still be tough to sort fact from myth when it comes to the Negro Leagues.

But we know that Gibson won nine home run titles for the Grays and Pittsburgh Crawfords, the most of any Negro Leagues player. And we know that, while playing in major-league parks, Gibson cracked homers at a rate comparable or superior to Babe Ruth.

Gibson, for example, hit 14 home runs in 107 at-bats in 1936, 18 in 82 AB in 1939, and 18 in 146 AB in 1946. And we know he hit .412 in autumn barnstorming tours against major leaguers.

We also know those tours were the closest Gibson got to the majors. The Senators and Pirates reportedly considered giving him tryouts in the late 1930s, but balked.

Gibson was a huge draw and a celebrity, enjoying the company of Duke Ellington, Lena Horne, and the Mills Brothers when the seemingly endless Negro Leagues tours reached big cities. But he was also a mysterious person who led a troubled and unsettled life away from the ballpark. His wife died giving birth to twins when she and Gibson were just teenagers. He suffered from high blood pressure and a brain tumor. And he died young in 1947, at the age of 35.

No. 1
JIMMIE FOXX
415

No. 2
LOU GEHRIG
347

No. 3
MEL OTT
308

No. 4
WALLY BERGER
241

No. 5
CHUCK KLEIN
238

No. 6
EARL AVERILL
218

No. 7
HANK GREENBERG
206

No. 8
BABE RUTH
198

No. 9
AL SIMMONS
190

No. 10
BOB JOHNSON
186

MOST HOME RUNS

1930 1939

hit only nine of his 29 dingers at Fenway in 1919) to the Polo Grounds. Clean, new balls were in the air. And the keepers of the game were willing to embrace a new hero instead of legislating against him.

It was bombs away from the first day the Babe put on pinstripes: 54 home runs with an OPS of 1.382 in 1920, then 59 taters and a 1.359 OPS the following season.

Best of all in terms of baseball's appeal in the now-Roaring Twenties, overall scoring started to rise, from 3.64 runs per team per game in the AL in 1918 to 4.76 in 1920 to 5.2 in 1925.

TWO EXTRA-INNING HOME RUNS IN SAME GAME

VERN STEPHENS Browns 9/29/1943
WILLIE KIRKLAND Indians 6/14/1963
ART SHAMSKY Reds 8/12/1966
RALPH GARR Braves 5/17/1971
MIKE YOUNG Orioles 5/28/1987

MOST AT-BATS WITHOUT A HOMERUN, CAREER

TOMMY THEVENOW, a 23-year-old shortstop for the Cardinals, hit an inside-the-park home run off the Phillies' Lefty Taber on September 17, 1926. Five days later, he pulled off another inside-the-park job. In the 1926 World Series, Babe Ruth misplayed a Thevenow drive into yet another inside-the-park homer. And then, although he played for 12 more seasons, Thevenow never hit another dinger.

While the rest of the world was learning to hit for power, Thevenow went the final 3,347 at-bats of his career without hitting a home run. That's the longest consecutive streak of homerless at-bats in history.

The second-longest belongs to Eddie Foster, a fine hit-and-run man who didn't hit a home run in 3,278 at-bats from April 1916 through the end of his career in 1923. His last homer before the streak came on an inside-the-parker, with President Woodrow Wilson in attendance. Foster's rate of 0.106 homers per 100 at-bats—he hit a total of six in a career that began in 1912—is the lowest of any player with 5,000 or more career at-bats.

Bill Holbert, a catcher in the 1880s, was also allergic to taters. Playing in a dozen seasons, he never hit a home run; his 2,335 at-bats are the most for a dingerless career.

No list of anti-sluggers would be complete without mention of Duane Kuiper, who played more than 1,000 games for Cleveland and San Francisco in the 1970s and 1980s, but hit just one home run in his career.

"One is better than none," he said after his lone blast, off Steve Stone of the White Sox on August 29, 1977. "But any more than that and people start expecting them."

There's a familiar stat that the Babe alone out-hit many teams in 1920 and 1921, and Ruth truly was a dominant player. More important, though, he was a one-man tipping point who demonstrated that players could consistently hit for power, that the long ball was not a freak of nature—more a Roger Bannister than a Wilt Chamberlain.

Other great players in the 1920s and 1930s—Rogers Hornsby, Lou Gehrig, Jimmie Foxx—approached Ruth's numbers and sometimes posted totals comparable to his. Even some players who weren't so great—Hack Wilson, Ken Williams—did. Meanwhile, home run totals went up across baseball, kept going up as more players emulated Ruth, and stayed high until World War II.

Ruth's impact extended to every area of baseball, even corners not commonly associated with his influence. He made big money—

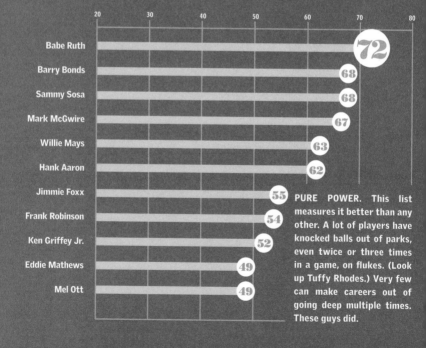

MOST GAMES WITH MULTIPLE HOME RUNS, CAREER

Babe Ruth	72
Barry Bonds	68
Sammy Sosa	68
Mark McGwire	67
Willie Mays	63
Hank Aaron	62
Jimmie Foxx	55
Frank Robinson	54
Ken Griffey Jr.	52
Eddie Mathews	49
Mel Ott	49

PURE POWER. This list measures it better than any other. A lot of players have knocked balls out of parks, even twice or three times in a game, on flukes. (Look up Tuffy Rhodes.) Very few can make careers out of going deep multiple times. These guys did.

HOME RUN
BROWN

WILLARD "HOME RUN" BROWN had just one home run in his major league career. It showed how far baseball had come—and how very far it still had to go.

Brown, who grew up in Shreveport, Louisiana, signed with the Kansas City Monarchs in 1935 for a $250 bonus, a salary of $125 a month, and $1 a day for meal money. He soon developed into one of black baseball's best sluggers and the Monarchs became the premier team in the Negro American League, which played in the western states.

From 1937 to 1948, Brown led the NAL in homers seven times and won batting titles in 1937, 1938, and 1941. Josh Gibson, the only man to lead the league more frequently in dingers than Brown, nicknamed him Home Run for outslugging Gibson when they went head to head.

An outfielder with speed and an above-average arm, Brown swung a 40-ounce bat, and he swung it at anything. He was also a fun-loving guy whose ease of manner suggested to some observers that he wasn't always playing at full speed.

"Willard was called a Sunday player because he played best when the stands were full," said catcher Sammy Haynes. Buck O'Neil, who played with and managed Brown, said, "This was the difference between Willard Brown and Jackie Robinson. Jackie looked like he was doing something, Willie Mays looked like he was doing something. Hank Aaron never did. And this was Willard. Everything came so easy for him."

Brown spent two years in the Army, landing in Normandy with the Quartermaster Corps. In 1945, he homered off Ewell Blackwell to help the Overseas Invasion Service Expedition beat the 71st Infantry Division in the G.I. World Series, which took place in Nuremberg, Germany, and featured black and white soldiers playing with and against each other.

On July 17, 1947, the St. Louis Browns purchased the contracts of Brown and his Monarchs teammate Hank Thompson. Jackie Robinson and Larry Doby had already entered the major leagues with a splash, but Brown had a far different experience. He went straight to St. Louis without spending time in the minors, and had a miserable time with a miserable team.

On August 13, Brown connected for an inside-the-parker off future Hall of Famer Hal Newhouser of the Tigers, marking the first American League homer by a black player. But Brown had used a bat that St. Louis' Jeff Heath discarded after part of its knob broke off, and even though he no longer had use for the lumber, Heath became enraged when he found out. So Heath broke the bat into pieces as Brown returned to the dugout, literally shattering Brown's moment.

Five weeks into what was essentially nothing more than a publicity stunt, Brown was hitting .179 in 21 games, and was released.

Brown picked up another moniker in Puerto Rico, where he became one of the mightiest sluggers winter ball has ever seen. He was called El Hombre after he won three home run titles and three batting crowns from 1946 through 1950. He won two Triple Crowns (1947–48 and 1949–50).

An eight-time All-Star in the Negro Leagues, Brown played four years for Dallas in the AA Texas League late in his career. He hit .300 with power until he was 40, led teams to pennants in 1953 and 1954, and was a local favorite. He lived the rest of his life in Houston, passing away in 1996.

Brown was elected to the Hall of Fame in February 2006.

"HOMER IN THE GLOAMIN'"

by *JOHN P. CARMICHAEL*

From the *Chicago Daily News*, September 29, 1938

THE PITTSBURGH PIRATES entered September 1938 leading the NL by six and half games, with the Chicago Cubs stuck in fourth. But over the next month, Chicago surged, and after Dizzy Dean beat the Pirates on September 27, Pittsburgh's lead was just half a game.

The next afternoon, with 34,465 fans shoehorned into Wrigley Field, the game was tied, 5-5, as the sun began to set. The umpires announced that if the contest wasn't settled by the end of the ninth, it would be called on account of darkness.

Up to the plate, with two outs and nobody on in the bottom of the ninth, strode Charles Leo "Gabby" Hartnett, in the 17th season of a Hall-of-Fame career. He saw three straight curveballs. The first he swung at and missed. The second he fouled off. The third he drove into the leftfield bleachers.

Hartnett's dinger, known forevermore as the "Homer in the Gloamin'," was celebrated the next day by John P. Carmichael in the *Chicago Daily News*:

We surrender to inadequacy. This Cub–Pirate pennant series has gone beyond our poor power to picture in words. When you squirm to fashion the pinnacle for Dizzy Dean, only to find you need at least its twin that a Gabby Hartnett may also brush the stars, word-painting becomes a magic art not given to the mine run of mortals to diffuse.

So let this be, today, a confession of helplessness to treat an afternoon that beggars description; an afternoon in the life of a stout-hearted Irishman who, as darkness almost wrapped around him from the sight of 35,000 quaking fans, changed the map of the baseball world with one devastating blow ...

For the second successive night, we stood in a clubhouse of crazed men in play suits. We can still see 'em fighting for words, staring at one another with glazed eyes. We can still see 'em pushing Hartnett from wall to wall with the irresistible force of robots gone wild. We can see Gabby trying vainly to free himself from his idolatrous teammates.

We can still see Billy Herman standing in the middle of the floor, arms akimbo. When he could talk, it was first just a whisper of awe: "Lord God Almighty." ... Then the full realization of the terrific sight he had just watched in the twilight smote him: "Lord God ALMIGHTY!" he suddenly screamed and threw his glove he knew not where.

The Cubs went on to win the pennant, only to be swept by the Yankees in four games. No matter. The 1938 Cubs, like the 1967 Red Sox and the 1973 Mets, were a team whose pennant race triumph turned the World Series into a big, fat anticlimax.

$80,000 by 1930—and his salary dragged pay upward for other players. His success with the Yankees made a genius out of Ed Barrow, who had moved from manager of the Red Sox to GM of the Yankees and acquired the Babe. And Barrow's corporate structure, which separated his front office from the team's ownership as well as from its field manager, became a model for other franchises. So did his tactic of plundering poorer teams for talent.

The home run revolution even changed the structure of ballparks. In 1920, the Yankees doubled their home attendance to more than 1.2 million, which got other clubs thinking about how to accommodate new fans. By then, most stadiums were in urban neighborhoods, so teams had to fill in the space they already had, adding outfield bleachers or grandstands along foul lines. For example, as Leonard Koppett, a longtime writer for the *New York Times*, once pointed out, when Ebbets Field first opened in 1913, it seated 18,000 fans with a grandstand ending just beyond third base, and had a leftfield fence that was 419 feet from home plate, along a street. Leftfield bleachers were installed in 1926, bringing the capacity to 28,000 but making the leftfield foul line 384 feet. Five years later, the Dodgers wrapped the grandstand all the way around leftfield, and later added box seats in

left. So by the time Gil Hodges and Roy Campanella were taking aim at Ebbets Field's leftfield wall, it was only 343 feet away—and the park could hold 32,000 fans.

It's easy to assume that home runs simply boost attendance, but the two stats actually have a circular relationship. Adding on to the park to accommodate the fans turbo-charged the home run boom ... which brought in still more fans.

All the while, the man they called The Sultan of Swat routinely crushed balls farther than fans had ever seen on his way to leading the league in homers 12 times and slugging percentage 13 straight years. Ruth was the first man to hit 30 home runs in a season— and the first to hit 40, 50, and 60. He was the first player to hit 300 career home runs—and the first to reach 400, 500, 600, and 700.

Now, about that home run Ruth "called" in Game 3 of the 1932 World Series ...

According to Ruthian mythology, bolstered by the Babe's own autobiography, in response to the merciless taunting of the Cubs and their lemon-tossing fans, he pointed to the outfield, then deposited a dinger in Wrigley Field's centerfield bleachers. Film evidence is inconclusive.

But only one of the many sportswriters covering the game, Joe Williams of the *New*

PART II

DEATH

by

HOME RUN

HOME RUNS may have been contributing factors in two famous baseball suicides.

In the summer of 1940, with Cincinnati driving toward its second straight NL pennant, Reds backup catcher Willard Hershberger had to fill in for an injured Ernie Lombardi. On July 31 at the Polo Grounds, Cincinnati ace Bucky Walters took a 4-1 lead into the bottom of the ninth inning and was one strike away from finishing off the Giants against four consecutive hitters.

But Bob Seeds walked, Burgess Whitehead went deep, Mel Ott walked, and Harry "The Horse" Danning, swinging from the heels, hit another home run to win the game.

A distraught Hershberger blamed himself for calling the wrong pitches. Three days later, in his room at the Copley Plaza Hotel, Hershberger slit his throat.

On October 12, 1986, the Angels were ahead of the Red Sox in the ALCS three games to one and leading the fifth game, 5-2, as the ninth inning started. Then Bill Buckner singled and Don Baylor homered, and by the time Donnie Moore came in to face Dave Henderson, the score was 5-4.

Henderson had entered the game in the fifth when Tony Armas was hurt. In the sixth, he bungled a Bobby Grich fly ball into a home run. But with one man on and two out, Henderson bopped a home run to left-field to keep Boston's season alive.

The Angels then tied the game in the bottom of the ninth, but in the 11th, Henderson hit a sacrifice fly, again off Moore, and Boston went on to win the game and the series.

On July 18, 1989, Moore shot his wife dead and then killed himself.

Obviously, anyone who kills himself has problems that go far beyond baseball. Hershberger had exhibited signs of paranoia and hypochondria, and had a family history of suicide. Moore had battled depression. In each sad instance, the intensity of the home run magnified the player's perception of his own failure.

In purely baseball terms, as is so often the case with history's goats, neither man deserved all the blame he placed on himself.

For instance, Angels reliever Gary Lucas hit the only batter he faced just before Henderson came to bat, and veteran Doug DeCinces managed only a shallow ball to right with the bases loaded, one out, and the score tied 6-6 in the bottom of the ninth.

And Hershberger's miscues were barely a speed bump for the 1940 Reds, who wound up winning the World Series—after which his teammates voted a full winner's share ($5,803.62) to his widowed mother, Maude.

York World-Telegram, described Ruth as pointing to centerfield that day, and in 1950 Williams said he wasn't sure anymore what Ruth's gesture meant.

Cubs pitcher Charlie Root always insisted he would have knocked Ruth flat had Babe pointed to the outfield. That seems likely. Chicago catcher Gabby Hartnett claimed Ruth was pointing to the Cubs' bench, saying, "It only takes one hit." That also seems reasonable. Ruth's homer may not have been forecast, but as a reply to Chicago, it was even better than Babe's comment on Wrigley Field: "I'd play for half my salary if I could hit in this dump all my life."

On the other hand, Ruth really did visit a little boy in the hospital, though here the facts also quickly grew into quasi-legend.

Eleven-year-old Johnny Sylvester of the Bronx was seriously injured after falling off a horse before the 1926 World Series, and when a friend of the family brought him balls signed by various Yankees and Cardinals who were about to square off for the World Championship, he also conveyed a get-well message from Ruth, who said he would hit a home run for Johnny. As it turned out, Ruth smacked four homers in the Series, and then visited a still-hospitalized but very happy Sylvester.

Arthur Daley, a sportswriter and columnist

MOST BIRTHDAY HOME RUNS

THE FIRST GREAT Polish-American ballplayer, and a man so intense he actually enjoyed rooming with Ty Cobb, Al Simmons went yard five times on his birthday, May 22. The last blast came in 1935 when he was 32.

A Hall of Famer, Simmons delivered a series of huge hits for Connie Mack's Philadelphia A's in the late 1920s and early 1930s. For instance, in Game 4 of the 1929 World Series, the Athletics were trailing the Cubs, 8-0, when Simmons led off the seventh inning with a towering homer onto the roof over the leftfield stands in Philly's Shibe Park. The A's proceeded to bat around, and Simmons singled and eventually scored the go-ahead run. Philadelphia won, 10-8, and went on to win the World Series in five games.

On Memorial Day, 1930, Simmons jacked a three-run homer in the ninth inning to tie the first game of a doubleheader against the Senators. He then doubled and scored the winning run in the 13th, but hurt his knee as he rounded third base. Forced to sit out the start of the second game, Simmons came off the bench with the A's trailing 7-4 in the fourth inning and pinch-hit a grand slam, sparking a 15-11 Philadelphia win.

Jimmie Foxx was the principal power source on those potent Philadelphia teams, but Simmons was a worthy no.2—and the indisputable no. 1 birthday hitter.

Al Simmons	Alex Rodriguez	13 other players
5	5	4

PINCH-HIT HOMERS IN BOTH GAMES OF A DOUBLEHEADER

- - - - - - - - - - - - - - - - - - - -

JOE CRONIN, player-manager and former All-Star shortstop for the Red Sox, cracked a three-run pinch-hit homer in the seventh inning of the first game of a doubleheader on June 17, 1943, against the Philadelphia A's, leading Boston to a 5-4 win. In the second game, Cronin sent himself up to the plate as a pinch-hitter again, this time in the eighth inning. He smacked another three-run dinger, although this time Boston lost, 8-7. This was the first time a pinch-hitter went deep in both halves of a twin bill.

The only player to match the feat since is Hal Breeden, a Montreal first-baseman, who did it for the Expos in a split doubleheader against the Braves on July 13, 1973. The Expos won the first game 11-7; the Braves copped the nightcap 15-6.

for *The New York Times*—usually a clear-eyed witness to history—insisted he saw Ruth slam a ball so hard that it zoomed back toward the mound, went through pitcher Hod Lisenbee's legs and then went over the head of charging centerfielder Tris Speaker for an inside-the-park home run.

It might be good to stop there, with gravity as well as logic being defied by a Ruthian feat. But it doesn't stretch credulity to point out that Ruth was so huge that he made an impact even when he played games that didn't count.

In 1924, the Yankees were able to acquire centerfielder Earle Combs from the minor league Louisville Colonels by offering them $50,000, a couple of players—and a promise that the Bombers would play an exhibition game in Louisville with Ruth in the lineup.

On October 17, 1926, Ruth hit 36 balls into a local river during a barnstorming off-season tour in Montreal with the Babe Ruth All-Stars; the game he was in was stopped because there were no balls left to play with. Six days later, the

HOME RUNS BY DAY OF THE WEEK

- -

S	M	T	W	TH	F	S
17.5% 41,268	10.4% 24,541	14.5% 34,240	14.5% 34,017	11.6% 27,247	15.2% 35,804	16.2% 38,228

MONDAY AND THURSDAY have always been post- and pre-weekend travel days for baseball teams, but there's another explanation for why so many dingers used to be hit on the "Lord's Day": Sunday doubleheaders.

Nowadays, doubleheaders are scheduled almost exclusively to make up rain dates, and there's less reason to expect more dingers on weekends than any other day of the week.

GREATEST
ALL★STAR GAME
Home Run

THE MOST FAMOUS home run in All-Star game history was a three-run, ninth-inning shot by Ted Williams at Detroit's Briggs Stadium that gave the American League a 7-5 win in 1941. Video tributes to Williams show the young Red Sox star clapping his hands and jumping for joy as he rounded the bases.

The most dramatic All-Star home run, however, was swatted by George "Mule" Suttles. Suttles, born in 1901, played for the Birmingham Black Barons before joining the St. Louis Stars in 1926. He led the Stars to the Negro National League championships in 1928, 1930, and 1931 with titanic shots that rivaled Josh Gibson's. And in the 1935 Negro Leagues All-Star game, called the East-West Game, Gibson batted fourth and Suttles fifth for the West.

The contest was tied, 8-8, when Gibson, already four for five, entered the batter's box in the bottom of the 11th. Suttles, hitless until then, called for a pitcher to come out and kneel in the on-deck circle, hoping that East pitcher Martin Dihigo would see the replacement and intentionally walk Gibson.

The trick worked. Gibson was given a free pass, whereupon Suttles took his turn at bat and won the game by clobbering a three-run opposite-field home run into the upper deck in rightfield at Chicago's Comiskey Park—the kind of stuff legends are made of.

Suttles' blast came on the Negro Leagues' biggest stage. The East-West Game, launched in 1933, was for a time the preeminent sporting event in black America, attracting top celebrities such as Louis Armstrong, Count Basie, and Joe Louis. Staged annually in Chicago, the East-West Game drew larger crowds than the major league All-Star game 10 times over the years.

All-time leaders on Negro Leagues lists change as research keeps digging deeper, but Suttles was one of black baseball's top three career home run hitters, along with Gibson and Turkey Stearnes.

Suttles played from age 17 until he was 42, and later had stints as a manager and umpire. He was elected to the Hall of Fame in February 2006.

"Don't worry about the Mule going blind," he once said about his own long career. "Just load the wagon and give me the lines."

Ted Williams, 1939–1942, 1946–1960
Frank Robinson, 1956–1976

No. 4T
15

No. 1T
18

Babe Ruth, 1914–1935
Mel Ott, 1926–1947
Hank Aaron, 1954–1976

No. 6T
13

No. 12T
14

Rogers Hornsby, 1915–1937
Lou Gehrig, 1923–1939
Willie Mays, 1951–1973
Barry Bonds, 1986–

Sam Crawford, 1899–1917
Jimmie Foxx, 1925–1942, 1944–1945
Mickey Mantle, 1951–1968
Harmon Killebrew, 1954–1975
Reggie Jackson, 1967–1987
Mike Schmidt, 1972–1989

MOST TIMES IN LEAGUE TOP-10 IN HOME RUNS

IN THE RIGHT ballpark and with a little luck, just about any slugger can win a home run title on a fluke—just look up Ripper Collins or Bill Melton in your *ESPN Baseball Encyclopedia*. Finishing among the top 10 homer hitters several times, though—that's a whole different kettle of taters.

The same is true, of course, for any statistical category. Lead it once, you give us a snapshot of a season; lead it many times, you paint a portrait of a career. Also, looking at league leaders automatically adjusts for the fact that home runs are harder to hit, on average, in some eras than in others. Reggie Jackson's 27 dingers in 1976 might not seem impressive at first glance, but they placed him second in the AL, just as Babe Ruth's 41 did in 1932.

There are two factors this list—in some ways, the most important in the book—doesn't account for.

One is home/road splits. Mel Ott hit 63 percent of his homers at the Polo Grounds, where the righfield fence was 258 feet down the line. Ott perfected the pull-jerk down the line out of necessity; the horseshoe-shaped Polo Grounds jumped sharply out to 440 in right-center.

Ted Williams, on the other hand, hit just 48 percent of his homers at Fenway Park, where the right-center power alley was 380. Down the line at Fenway was only a little over 300, but Williams—ever a purist—refused to adjust his power stroke to suit local conditions.

The other is quality of competition. It's easier to dominate leagues when talent is thinner, as it was, say, before integration.

But leading the league multiple times is impressive no matter what the era. That's why every slugger on this list is—or, in Barry Bonds' case, will be—in the Hall of Fame.

All-Stars reached South Bend, Indiana, and found the locals had purchased a batch of baseballs for $1.23 each in anticipation of Ruth's visit.

In September 1931, Ruth participated in a three-way benefit series among the Yankees, Giants, and Dodgers to raise money for the unemployed. Between games, the left-handed Babe took part in the fungo contest as a right-handed batter—and proceeded to blast a shot 421 feet, breaking the 20-year-old fungo-hitting distance record.

Okay, one more example from a real game. On July 4, 1921, Ruth hit a towering infield fly that shot up to about twice the height of the facade of the Polo Grounds, until it was barely visible against the bright blue sky. A's second baseman Jimmie Dykes circled and circled, waiting for the ball to come down. When it finally did plummet back to earth, Dykes lunged for the ball and missed it. Ruth pulled into second base, laughing.

Even the Babe's popups were titanic. And, of course, so were his appetites.

Ruth ate so prodigiously (he once reportedly devoured an 18-egg omelet) that his daily pre-game meal included bicarbonate of soda. He drank oceans of beer. He enthusiastically bedded as many women as he could get his hands on. Lieb, who once saw a woman chase after the Babe on a Pullman train car with a knife pointed at his back, speculated that Ruth might have been a reincarnated Babylonian phallus worshipper. Whether noisily having sex in hotel rooms for entire nights, bidding too aggressively at bridge, or driving golf balls as far as he could, Ruth spent nearly every waking minute consuming some physical experience.

YOUNGEST HR HITTER

JUST 17 YEARS and 257 days old, Tommy "Buckshot" Brown crunched a pitch from the Pirates' Preacher Roe into the leftfield stands at Ebbets Field on August 20, 1945, to become the youngest major leaguer to hit a home run.

And five days later, Buckshot became the second-youngest to hit a homer when he clocked a four-bagger against the Giants.

Brown came up with the Dodgers in 1944 when he was 16. He had a few wartime highlights—he's also the youngest player ever to steal home—but only played sporadically after Pee Wee Reese returned to the Dodgers from military service in 1946. Brown hung on with the Dodgers, Phillies, and Cubs through the 1953 season, when his nine-year major league career ended.

He was 25.

And nothing satisfied his appetites so much as clouting home runs.

Ruth's immense energy has often been interpreted as an expression of unbridled joy, and there's little doubt that the man knew how to have a good time. But Robert Creamer, the biographer who came to understand him best, hinted at something sadder in describing Ruth's affection for children: "With them, there were no rules, no authority, no need to apologize, to explain, to explode, to drink, to fuck, to prove himself over and over ... Like a child, he did not like to wait or plan for the right moment. He did not like to wait for anything. 'It might rain tomorrow,' he would say."

Thought of as living life as a race against boredom, for a long time Babe Ruth was actually on the run from emptiness. He never fulfilled his goal of managing after his playing days were over, and he died from throat cancer at the age of 53. It's hopeful to think but impossible to know whether his casually majestic talent brought him as much happiness as it did his fans.

MOST GAMES WITH MULTIPLE HOME RUNS, SEASON

11
HANK GREENBERG, 1938 Tigers
SAMMY SOSA, 1998 Cubs

10
JIMMIE FOXX, 1938 Red Sox
RALPH KINER, 1947 Pirates
MARK McGWIRE, 1998 Cardinals
BARRY BONDS, 2001 Giants
SAMMY SOSA, 2001 Cubs
ALEX RODRIGUEZ, 2002 Rangers

9
WILLIE MAYS, 1955 Giants
GEORGE BELL, 1987 Blue Jays
MARK McGWIRE, 1999 Cardinals
DAVID ORTIZ, 2005 Red Sox
ANDRUW JONES, 2005 Braves

Big and powerful as a teenager, Hank Greenberg grew up in the Bronx but was so clumsy and gawky that Giants manager John McGraw, who was always looking for a Jewish star in New York, passed on signing him.

GREENBERG SIGNED instead with Detroit, and cracked the Tigers lineup at the age of 22.

The first in a string of amazing slugging seasons came in 1934, when Greenberg socked 26 homers, knocked in 139 runs, and cracked a major league-leading 63 doubles for the pennant-winning Tigers. In 1935, he tied for the MLB lead in homers (36), led the majors in RBI (170), and earned MVP honors while leading Detroit to a World Championship.

Greenberg missed most of 1936 with injuries, but came back strong in 1937, hitting 40 homers and leading the majors with 183 RBI, the third-highest total ever. In 1938, he blasted 58 homers with 146 RBI. In 1939, he hit 33 homers with 112 RBI. And in 1940, Greenberg was the AL MVP again, batting .340 with 150 RBI.

All the while, Greenberg stared down anti-Semitism—sometimes of the most virulent sort, as when the Cubs rode him mercilessly during the 1935 World Series, and sometimes of the merely clueless variety, as when virtually every contemporary newspaper account felt obligated to note that he was Jewish or "Hebrew."

In the heat of the 1934 pennant race,

Greenberg had to decide whether to play against Boston on Rosh Hashanah, the Jewish New Year. "I came from Kansas and I never knew what a Jew was," said Elden Auker, Detroit's starting pitcher that day. "The papers said Hank wasn't going to play because it was a Jewish holiday. That's when I found out what Rosh Hashanah was."

Greenberg played. He hit two home runs, the second in the bottom of the ninth to win the game, 2-1. Auker was the winning pitcher. The next day, the front-page headline in the Detroit Free Press was "Happy New Year, Hank"—in Yiddish.

(Yom Kippur, a solemn holiday, would have presented Greenberg with a more serious dilemma, but the Tigers had the AL flag sewed up by the time it arrived, so he sat out.)

Greenberg's biggest home run season was 1938, when his 11th multiple-dinger game of the year, on September 27, brought him to 58 with five games to play. He went homerless the rest of the way.

Drafted into military service just 19 games into the 1941 season, Greenberg was discharged on December 5, two days before Pearl Harbor. He immediately re-enlisted. Green-

HANK GREENBERG STATS

Year	Team	G	R	HR	RBI	BB	AVG	OPS
1930	Tigers	1	0	0	0	0	.000	.000
1933	Tigers	117	59	12	87	46	.301	.835
1934	Tigers	153	118	26	139	63	.339	1.005
1935	Tigers	152	121	36	170	87	.328	1.039
1936	Tigers	12	10	1	16	9	.348	1.085
1937	Tigers	154	137	40	183	102	.337	1.105
1938	Tigers	155	144	58	146	119	.315	1.122
1939	Tigers	138	112	33	112	91	.312	1.042
1940	Tigers	148	129	41	150	93	.340	1.103
1941	Tigers	19	12	2	12	16	.269	.872
1945	Tigers	78	47	13	60	42	.311	.948
1946	Tigers	142	91	44	127	80	.277	.977
1947	Pirates	125	71	25	74	104	.249	.885
	Career Totals	1394	1051	331	1276	852	.313	1.017

berg didn't make it back to the big leagues until midway through the 1945 season. He banged a homer his first game back, and hit a grand slam on the final day of the season as Detroit edged Washington for the pennant.

In 1946, Greenberg led the majors in HR (44) and the AL in RBI (127). But Tigers owner Walter Briggs, who never particularly liked his star slugger and didn't approve of his front office ambitions, balked at boosting his $75,000 salary. Briggs put him on waivers—Greenberg learned of the move on the radio—and he ended up in Pittsburgh.

Greenberg played one season with the Pirates, where he became baseball's first $100,000-a-year player and mentor to the young Ralph Kiner, who credits Greenberg with helping him develop as a player and a person.

Greenberg was hired in 1948 by Indians owner Bill Veeck as farm system director; two years later, he became Cleveland's GM. Greenberg followed Veeck to the White Sox in 1959 as a part-owner, but left baseball in 1963 to become an investment banker.

A strong personality who insisted on pur-

suing his own ideas—as early as 1935 he had his gloves custom made, with extra webbing between thumb and mitt—Greenberg was always an outsider.

Significantly, the world he was born into never let him or anyone else forget his faith. Newspapers in the 1930s covered Greenberg, Jewish ballplayers, and Jews in general almost as members of a different species—not necessarily negative, but definitely apart.

Not surprisingly, Greenberg supported another outsider, Jackie Robinson, when Robinson broke the color barrier in 1947. He worked for Veeck, the most iconoclastic owner ever. And he testified on behalf of Curt Flood when Flood sued to overturn baseball's reserve clause.

Twelve years after his death at the age of 75, Greenberg was the subject of a loving, revelatory documentary released in 1998 called *The Life and Times of Hank Greenberg*, which won a George Foster Peabody for Broadcast Excellence.

It's the best documentary ever made about a home run hitter.

HANK GREENBERG

CHAPTER 3

1946-1962

★

Home Run

Hitters

DRIVE CADILLACS

★ ★ ★

Baseball after World War II

was a golden age that gave us Willie, Mickey, and the Duke. It also gave us
Eddie (Mathews), Ralph (Kiner), and Big Klu (Ted Kluszewski), three more
of a generation of sluggers whose bats would lift the game with home runs
for more than a decade.

MICKEY MANTLE

The postwar power

show actually started before the end of World War II (but seven weeks after V-E Day) on July 1, 1945, when Hank Greenberg returned to Detroit for the first time in more than four years. The original Hammerin' Hank smacked a home run off Charlie Gassaway, helping the Tigers beat the Athletics and leaving 47,700 fans delirious. On September 30, the last day of the season, Greenberg hit a grand slam in the bottom of the ninth inning to beat the Browns 6-3 and clinch the pennant for the Tigers.

The big boys were back in town. And with them came a series of developments that sent balls over fences at rates baseball wouldn't see again until the bulked-up 1990s.

Most important, Jackie Robinson and the Dodgers broke the color line in 1947, and along with all-around performers like Robinson, power hitters such as Larry Doby, Roy Campanella, and Luke Easter hit the big leagues, soon followed by Willie Mays, Ernie Banks, and Hank Aaron.

In his autobiography, Aaron observes that had there been no black players in the National League, Ron Santo would have led the NL in home runs during the 1960s by a margin of nearly 50. His point: It was obviously easier for great white players such as Babe Ruth to dominate the game in the years before integration. And it's true that Major League Baseball's talent level has never risen so sharply in a short period as it did in the seasons following Robinson's arrival.

Moreover, that talent wasn't evenly distributed. You know how football used to have an unofficial "no black quarterbacks" rule? After not even the most extreme racist could deny the talent of black athletes, it still took most football teams—college and pro—years to believe they could

CONTINUED ON PAGE 66

No. 1
TED WILLLIAMS
234

No. 2
JOHNNY MIZE
217

No. 3
BILL NICHOLSON
211

No. 4
RUDY YORK
189

No. 5
JOE GORDON
181

No. 6
JOE DiMAGGIO
180

No. 7
VERN STEPHENS
177

No. 8
CHARLIE KELLER
173

No. 9
RALPH KINER
168

No. 10
BOBBY DOERR
164

MOST HOME RUNS
1940 **1949**

No. 3
6TH INNING TO
LEFT FIELD OFF
BOB SAVAGE

BOBBY LOWE Beaneaters, 5/30/1894	
ED DELAHANTY Phillies, 7/13/1896	
LOU GEHRIG Yankees, 6/3/1932	
CHUCK KLEIN Phillies, 7/10/1936	
PAT SEEREY White Sox, 7/18/1948	
GIL HODGES Dodgers, 8/31/1950	
JOE ADCOCK Braves, 7/31/1954	
ROCKY COLAVITO Indians, 6/10/1959	
WILLIE MAYS Giants, 4/30/1961	
MIKE SCHMIDT Phillies, 4/17/1976	
BOB HORNER Braves, 7/6/1986	
MARK WHITEN Cardinals, 9/7/1993	
MIKE CAMERON Mariners, 5/2/2002	
SHAWN GREEN Dodgers, 5/23/2002	
CARLOS DELGADO Blue Jays, 9/25/2003	

"The definitive player of the era"—that's how Bill James characterized **Pat Seerey**, citing the journeyman outfielder's stat line in 1948, when he hit just .231 and struck out 102 times but also swatted 19 homers, drove in 70 runs, and drew 68 walks in only 105 games. Seerey had a bunch of seasons like that—in 1944, 1945, 1946, and 1948, he finished in the top 10 in the AL in dingers while leading the league in strikeouts.

The Indians brought Seerey up during World War II and stuck with him through four seasons of strikeouts and fielding misadventures. Seerey had legitimate power,

FOUR HOME RUNS

★ *in One Game* ★

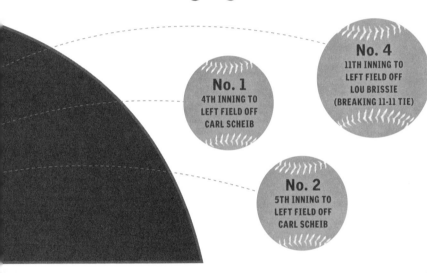

No. 1
4TH INNING TO
LEFT FIELD OFF
CARL SCHEIB

No. 2
5TH INNING TO
LEFT FIELD OFF
CARL SCHEIB

No. 4
11TH INNING TO
LEFT FIELD OFF
LOU BRISSIE
(BREAKING 11-11 TIE)

but was baffled by big-league curveballs. In 1947, Indians owner Bill Veeck hired Rogers Hornsby to tutor Seerey for eight weeks before spring training. It didn't help: Seerey wound up hitting .171.

Seerey was traded to the last-place White Sox in June 1948, and entered the record books six weeks later. In the first game of a doubleheader against the Athletics at Shibe Park in Philadelphia, he actually hit a curveball out of the park in the fourth inning, then followed up with homers in the fifth, sixth, and eleventh, the last one breaking an 11-11 tie to win the game.

A local business happened to be offering $500 to any player who hit four home runs in a single game—the feat had been accomplished only four times before. Seerey got his money the next day.

Sportswriters dug up Bobby Lowe, who'd been the first batter to smack four homers in a game 54 years earlier. Lowe's take: "He weighs more than 200 pounds! Why, that would almost make two of me!"

Seerey was released by Chicago in 1949 after appearing in four games (0 for 4). He retired at the age of 26, still unable to hit a curveball.

entrust a visible position of on-field leadership to black players. There was a corollary in baseball: The major leagues admitted and developed few black starting pitchers in the two decades after Robinson arrived on the scene. (To this day, only 13 blacks have won 20 games in a big-league season.)

At the same time, players of every stripe, from Yankee Stadium to the sandlots, were busy adopting the Ruthian tactic of swinging for the fences, holding the bat near its handle and whipping it like a golf club to generate maximum power. When Ralph Kiner was once advised to choke up, he replied, "Cadillacs are down at the end of the bat." (It was a teammate, Pirates pitcher Fritz Ostermueller, who said, "Home-run hitters drive Cadillacs," a more famous phrase often attributed to Kiner.)

And over time, hitters discovered they could get even more leverage by using lighter bats. In Ruth's day players wielded mace-like clubs weighing more than 40 ounces. But

10 MANTLE MOONSHOTS

0 .... 50 .... 100 .... 150 .... 200 .... 250 .... 300 3

FROM HIS FIRST SPRING TRAINING with the Yankees, Mickey Mantle launched home runs that became legends for the enormous distances they traveled.

Mantle was still trying to make the team in March 1951 when **1** in an exhibition game against college players, he catapulted a home run that flew out of USC's Bovard Field and over an adjacent football field.

On April 17, 1953, **2** Mantle jacked one of the most famous home runs in history, bashing a Chuck Stobbs fastball out of Washington's Griffith Stadium. The ball sailed over the left-center bleachers, clipped a beer sign but kept going over the adjacent street, then finally bounced into a backyard.

"That one's got to be measured!" yelled Red Patterson, the Yankees' public relations director, who witnessed Mantle's bomb. Patterson raced down from the press box, went out behind the bleachers looking for witnesses, and came up with a 10-year-old boy named Donald Dunaway who showed him where the ball had landed, a few houses up the block at 434 Oakdale Place. Patterson walked back along the ball's path and came up with a distance: 565 feet. Skeptics quibbled, but the story and the number made newspapers across the country—as did a photo of Mantle, Patterson, and a huge tape measure.

Just 11 days later, **3** Mantle hit another homer that cleared the leftfield wall in Sportsman's Park in St. Louis, rocketed across the street and hit the second-floor porch of a nearby house. On June 11, **4** he hit the right-field roof at Briggs Sta-

when Ernie Banks—who at 6'1", 180 pounds was built like Aaron—hit an unheard-of 44 homers as a shortstop in 1955, he did it with an unheard-of 30-ounce bat.

Teams were still moving in their fences, too—and not just to keep adding seats, but in the case of some enterprising executives, expressly to boost home runs. After Bill Veeck bought the Indians in 1946, he installed a storm fence across the outfield of cavernous Cleveland Municipal Stadium. This cut the distance in the power alleys by 70 feet, and home runs jumped 93 percent in 1948 (from 61 hit by the Indians and their opponents in 1946 to 118). When the Pirates acquired Greenberg in 1947, they added a fence 30 feet inside the leftfield wall at Forbes Field, creating an area known as Greenberg's Gardens. The gardens didn't help Greenberg much, but they did aid Kiner, who mashed 28 taters at home in 1947, then 31 in 1948 to justify the new name—Kiner's Korner.

565'

| 400 | 450 | 500 | 550 | 600 | 650 | 700 |

dium in Detroit, a location only Ted Williams had previously cleared. On July 6, **5** The Mick pinch-hit a grand slam over the second-deck roof in left-center field at Connie Mack Stadium in Philadelphia. On September 12, **6** he smashed a ball into the upper deck in leftfield at Yankee Stadium, destroying a seat some 80 feet above the field.

And all that was just in 1953.

Mantle routinely sent balls to places home runs had never visited before. In June 1955, **7** he crushed a Billy Pierce fastball that seemed to land in a light tower at Comiskey Park in Chicago. Attendants stationed on the roof later confirmed that the ball cleared the stadium entirely. At Yankee Stadium on Memorial Day, 1956, **8** he smacked a Pedro Ramos pitch off the upper deck facade of rightfield. In September

1960, **9** he sent a three-run job over the rightfield roof in Detroit that landed in the Brooks Lumber yard, across Trumbull St.

According to Mantle himself, the hardest ball he ever hit came on May 22, 1963, in the bottom of the 11th inning of a 7-7 game against the Kansas City A's. **10** Mantle sent a high fastball from pitcher Bill Fischer soaring on a high arc toward right field. On his way to first base, Mantle stopped to watch to see if it might become the first ball ever to exit Yankee Stadium, but it smacked the top of the decorative facade along the roof over the third deck.

Talking with the *New York Post*'s Maury Allen after the game, Mantle pronounced "facade" as "fuh-card," prompting Allen to write, "When you hit them as far as Mickey does, it hardly matters how you pronounce them."

"Trader Frank" Lane, GM of the White Sox, put up chicken wire at Comiskey Park, then tore it down when opposing hitters took advantage of the new dimensions. The Reds moved in their rightfield fences by 24 feet in 1953, and more than doubled the number of homers they hit (and allowed) at home, with Kluszewski jumping from 4 to 23 at Crosley Field. Until the mid-1950s, Griffith Stadium in Washington, D.C. was the toughest park on the planet to clear: The Senators hit an absurd total of 10 home runs at home in 1947 and again in 1953. But once the team started to develop sluggers, owner Calvin Griffith brought the fences in by up to 38 feet and his lineup tripled their homer output at home.

CLOTHES MAKE THE MAN

YOU HAVE TO GO PRETTY FAR DOWN the all-time list to find anyone known for his stylishness. Babe Ruth, Harmon Killebrew, and Jimmie Foxx could barely fit into suits. Ted Williams famously despised neckties. Sammy Sosa and Rafael Palmeiro got gussied up for congressional hearings, but not in a way that really caught the eye. Carl Yastrzemski (said Bill Lee) made Inspector Clouseau look good: "He had the same London Fog raincoat his entire career. We'd throw it in trash cans all around the league, and somehow it mysteriously made its way back."

One big-time power hitter known for his nattiness was Duke Snider, named one of the best-dressed men in America in 1955 by the Custom Tailors Guild of America. Others on the list that year included Clark Gable, Bob Hope, Richard Nixon, and Frank Sinatra. "It was flattering," Snider said, "especially considering that I didn't have that many clothes."

Snider's only serious competition among today's sluggers comes from Alex Rodriguez, whose sartorial style is of a piece with his perfectly composed persona. But the Duke gets the nod based on his endorsement power. By the mid-1950s, Snider was appearing in television spots for the Arthur Murray Dance School and Mayo Spruce undergarments, as well as for Gillette razors, Lucky Strike cigarettes, Ovaltine, and—unaccountably—crib mattresses at Gimbel's.

The 6'0", 190-pound Silver Fox had sufficient self-assurance to utter these words with aplomb: "On and off the diamond I like to feel free. Mayo Spruce underwear is all action—doesn't bind or bunch. Comfortable? And how! See for yourself—spruce up today!"

Who was the best-dressed slugger of all time?

The cumulative result: Balls went bye-bye like never before. Major-league hitters smashed 1,704 home runs, an all-time record, in 1949, then proceeded to set a new single-season mark the following season and again in 1953, 1955, and 1956, and in the expansion years of 1961 and 1962. Home runs became more important than batting average. League BAs, which had been above .270 before the war, drifted beneath .260, and in 1946, Greenberg became the second player in major-league history to clout more than 40 homers while hitting under .300. Stolen bases plunged from an overall total of 1,019 in 1937 to 760 in 1947, then fell again to 730 in 1949, and hit an all-time low of 650 in 1950.

The home run binge made some old-timers distinctly cranky. "Now they have gone to the hit per distance game. They look as though they will be lucky to hit .340 or maybe less," growled Ty Cobb in 1952. "The hit and run, stolen base, bunt and sacrifice are deteriorating from unuse, and they only hit for their amusement and pleasure for the home run."

Cobb was right, at least in the short term. Teams were playing "moneyball" 50 years before *Moneyball*.

At first, pitchers responded to the home run barrage with wildness born of sheer terror: AL hurlers walked more batters than they struck out every year from 1947 through 1951. Pitchers didn't regain their control until the end of the 1950s, when strikeouts were nearly 50 percent more common than walks.

Robin Roberts was a big reason for that. Year in and year out, the Phillies' ace was the best pitcher in the NL because even though he gave up buckets of homers—including a then-record 46 in 1956—he kept runners off the bases. Roberts led the league in dingers allowed five times during his

MOST HOME RUNS BY ONE BATTER OFF ONE PITCHER

19 Duke Snider
vs.
Robin Roberts

18 Willie Mays
vs.
Warren Spahn

17 Hank Aaron
vs.
Don Drysdale

17 Stan Musial
vs.
Warren Spahn

17 Babe Ruth
vs.
Rube Walberg

CONTINUED ON PAGE 73

TAPE-MEASURE TRIGONOMETRY

HOW DO YOU CALCULATE THE DISTANCE OF A HOME RUN?

WE LOVE NUMBERS. We're baseball fans, after all. And if you like a little mathematics, too, then get out your scientific calculator and fasten your seat belt. Otherwise, skip right on down to the final paragraph.

First things first: When we talk about home run distances, we're not discussing how far a ball flies before it hits a wall, a window, or a fan. Nor do we mean the overall length of its arc. We mean how far a ball would have gone if it had traveled without anything getting in its way before it landed on the ground.

Now, any object that is launched into the air—whether a baseball, an arrow, or a cannonball—travels in a parabolic arc, decelerates, then falls back to earth. And mathematically, all parabolas can be graphed using the following equation:

$$y = ax^2 + bx + c$$

Wherein a and b determine the parabola's size and shape, and c is the point at which the parabola intersects the graph's y axis.

Still reading? Okay then, suppose we superimpose a graph on the trajectory of a home run. Looking at the chart, you can see the point $(0, c)$ is where the batted ball is launched, (h,v) is where it hits an obstruction and $(d,0)$ is where it would have come to rest. To figure out what the home run's parabolic equation is, we can calculate d—the ball's "true" distance—by figuring out when $y = 0$.

One key piece of information in doing this is the ball's angle of impact, shown as angle Q in the chart. The tangent of this angle describes the slope of the home run's path at the moment of obstruction; it is equal to the vertical distance the ball has traveled (its "rise"), divided by the horizontal distance it has gone (its "run"). But calculus tells us that the slope of a curve is also the first derivative of that curve. So for our home run:

$$y = ax^2 + bx + c$$

$$y = ah^2 + bh + c$$

But also:
$$y' \text{ (or } dy/dx) = 2ax + b$$

So:
$$\tan(Q) = y' \text{ at } (h,v) = 2ah + b$$

Conduct a little algebraic shuffling on both sides of our original equation and we find:

$$a = \frac{h \tan(Q) + c - v}{h^2}$$

$$b = \frac{2v}{h} - \frac{2c}{h} - \tan(Q)$$

Once we have our values for a and b, we can use the quadratic formula we all learned in high school—you do remember that, don't you?—to determine the roots of the original parabolic equation. That is, what number solves the equation at $y = 0$. In this case, that will be our home run's distance.

$$x = \frac{-b \pm \sqrt{b^2 - 4ac}}{2a}$$

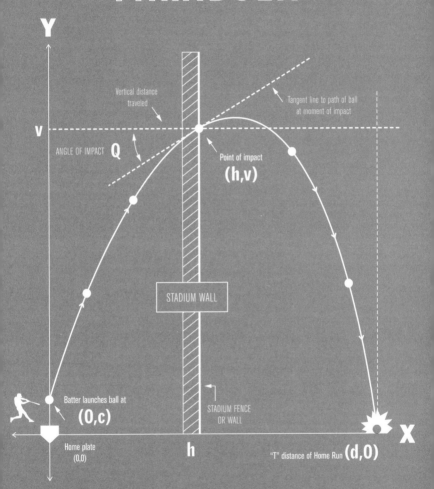

PARABOLA

Y

Vertical distance traveled

Tangent line to path of ball at moment of impact

v

ANGLE OF IMPACT **Q**

Point of impact
(h,v)

STADIUM WALL

Batter launches ball at
(0,c)

STADIUM FENCE
OR WALL

Home plate
(0,0)

h

"T" distance of Home Run **(d,0)**

X

horizontal distance traveled=h / vertical distance traveled=v

Piece of cake, right?

IN A FAMOUS LABELED PHOTO of the May 1963 home run that Mickey Mantle very nearly smashed out of Yankee Stadium, the ball is shown striking the top of the right-field facade 118 feet above the ground after traveling 370 feet on the fly. Using the Pythagorean Theorem, we can figure out that it traveled 351 feet horizontally. And Mantle probably hit the ball while it was about three feet off the ground. So:

- -

$$h = 351$$

$$v = 118$$

$$c = 3$$

- -

The ball was probably coming down slightly when it hit the facade, making the angle of impact 165 degrees (meaning it was sloping downward by 15 degrees). Then:

$$a = \frac{351 * \tan(165) + 3 - 118}{351^2}$$

$$a = -0.001697$$

$$b = \frac{2 * 118}{351} - \frac{2 * 3}{351} - \tan(165)$$

$$b = 0.9232$$

So our distance, the point (d,0) at which Mantle's home run parabola crosses the x-axis of the graph we have drawn, will be given by the solution to the equation:

$$y = ax^2 + bx + c$$

$$y = -0.001697x^2 + 0.9232x + 3$$

Using the quadratic formula, we find one positive solution:

$$x = 547.25t$$

Thus, Mantle's home run would have gone 547 feet. And three inches.

If you've come this far, you'll notice how much depends on the precise value of Q. The horizontal and vertical distances a home run ball travels are pretty easy to measure, but its angle of impact is more subjective. On the National Curve Bank, an Internet site for math students, Stewart Venit ran the numbers for Mantle's home run, assuming an angle of 150 degrees, and arrived at an estimate of 502 feet. On the other hand, the devotees who run Mantle's official website claim not only that the ball was still rising when it hit the facade, but that it would have kept rising for another 20 feet—which yields a distance of 734 feet! (Unfortunately, that number really isn't humanly possible.)

So now you know: Today's computerized cameras track a home-run ball's horizontal distance, its vertical elevation, and the angle at which it strikes whatever object stops it. And the rest, as chess players say, is a matter of technique. But unless you've got an accurate read on a home run's angle of impact, you can juggle exponents, tangents, and intercepts all day and the ball's unobstructed distance will still be in the eye of the beholder.

And guess what? Baseball has no official beholder: Some clubs use a crude formula for measuring HRs, some rely on eyeball estimates, some don't even bother.

Somehow, that's soothing.

career, but he also finished in the top three in WHIP (walks plus hits per inning pitched) nine times. He threw 300 innings a year over the entire decade of the 1950s by throwing strikes and living with the results, and his example gave others new resolve.

Meanwhile, homers came from players at every position, including those traditionally deemed more important for their fielding. Roy Campanella (41 HR in 1953), Banks (47 in 1958), and Eddie Mathews (47 in 1953) set single-season records for homers by a catcher, shortstop, and third baseman, respectively (though all have since been broken). Even pitchers got into the act. No 20th-century team had gotten more than 10 home runs from its moundsmen until the staffs of the 1949 Indians (led by Bob Lemon) and the 1955 Dodgers (Don Newcombe) belted 11, and then the 1956 White Sox (the otherwise forgotten Jack Harshman) smashed 12.

Gotham had Mantle, Mays, and Snider, but even fans of wretched teams had sluggers they could call their own. The names of Hank Sauer of the Cubs, Roy Sievers of the Senators, and Gus Zernial of the Philadelphia Athletics survive today at the level of cross-word puzzle clues, but they all had genuine power—enough for each to have led the league in homers. Sauer, in fact, was named

the NL's Most Valuable Player in 1952 while hitting .270; only Roger Maris (1961) and wartime winner Marty Marion (1944) have taken home an MVP trophy with a lower batting average for players who are not pitchers. Kiner played on some of the worst teams this side of the 1899 Cleveland Spiders, but grew famous enough to date Elizabeth Taylor and Janet Leigh. (Leigh left Ralph for Tony Curtis, who taught Kiner tricks he had learned while playing the role of Harry Houdini.)

And the home runs came in bunches. Three players had three-home-run games for the 1950 Dodgers (Snider, Campanella, and Gil Hodges, who hit four in his game). That accomplishment was surpassed by the 1956 Reds (Gus Bell, Ed Bailey, Bob Thurman, and Kluszewski) but matched by only three other teams. The 1952 Giants became the first club with nine players to hit at least 10 homers each, then repeated the feat six years later, after moving to San Francisco. Only twice before WWII had a team stocked five 20-homer hitters, but it happened three times in the 1950s—and then the 1961 Yankees offered up six in double digits.

All the homers and records called new attention to power statistics and generated a new level of celebrity for the hitters who compiled them. When the 1947 Giants

THE BALLAD OF *Rocky Nelson*

by RAYMOND SOUSTER
The Collected Poems of Raymond Souster (1959)

When old Rocky Nelson shuffles up to the plate
The outfield shifts round and the fans all wait.
He takes up his stance which ignores every law,
Has a last slow suck of the quid of his jaw,
And waits while the pitcher makes up his mind
What new deception his arm can unwind.
Then the ball comes in and the sound of wood
That's heard by the ear does the loyal heart good,
And the ball rises up like a hunted thing
Pursued by an angry bumble-bee sting,
And the outfielders run but it's no use at all —
Another one over the right field wall.
And as Rocky trots slowly around the bases
Happiness lights up twelve thousand faces.

BEST HOME RUN POEM

ROCKY NELSON was something of a minor-league legend, smashing 215 career homers while hitting .326 and picking up three International League MVPs. His big-league career spanned nine seasons over a 12-year period, with his best season coming in 1960, when he batted .300 with 7 HR and 35 RBI in part-time play for Pittsburgh.

The Pirates won the pennant that year, and Nelson was playing first base in the World Series against the Yankees as Pittsburgh tried to protect a 9-7 lead in the ninth inning of Game 7. In the first inning, Nelson hit a two-run homer to give the Pirates an early lead. But in the ninth, with two men on and nobody out, Mickey Mantle singled, scoring one and moving a runner to third. Then Yogi Berra hit a grounder to first. Nelson stepped on the base for the second out, but Mantle dodged Rocky's tag in getting back to first base, allowing the tying run to score.

Fortunately for Nelson and the Pirates, Bill Mazeroski, leading off the bottom of the ninth, drove a 1-0 pitch from Ralph Terry over the leftfield wall at Forbes Field for the only Game 7 walk-off home run in World Series history.

clubbed a record 221 homers, it just wasn't one of the biggest stories of the year. But by the time the 1956 Reds approached the mark, team members were well aware of its significance. On September 29, with Cincinnati sitting on 220 home runs, manager Birdie Tebbetts sent Smoky Burgess to pinch-hit for the pitcher in a game against Chicago.

"You know why I'm having you hit?" Tebbetts asked.

"You want me to hit a home run so we'll tie the record," Burgess replied.

"Right," said Tebbetts. "Homer or nothing."

Burgess cracked a home run onto Sheffield Avenue outside Wrigley Field.

Six years later, when Yogi Berra hit the Yankees' 221st home run of the 1961 season, Whitey Ford joked, "It'll make you famous as the guy whose homer tied the record." Of course, Roger Maris and Mickey Mantle gained all the ink that year as they waged an endlessly publicized and debated race to beat Ruth's single-season total of 60. The Yankees ended the season with 240 home runs, Mantle finished with 54 and Maris wound up with 61—and an ulcer.

In 1960, dingers got their own TV show with *Home Run Derby*, a half-hour syndicated program (in living black and white) sponsored by Gillette. The premise was simple: Top sluggers took turns trying to crack batting-practice pitches out of L.A.'s tiny Wrigley Field, with called strikes, swinging strikes, foul balls, and anything falling short of the fences counting as an out. The winner earned $2,000, the loser got $1,000, and anybody who went yard three straight times received a $500 bonus—nice chunks of change at a time when the biggest stars in the game were making less than $80,000 a year.

CONTINUED ON PAGE 80

GREAT STARTS

ON SEPTEMBER 14, 1951, Bob Nieman of the St. Louis Browns became the first player to hit a home run in his first two major-league at-bats when he smacked a pair of dingers off Red Sox lefty Mickey McDermott at Fenway Park. (Later in the game, Nieman beat out a bunt!) Eighty-nine other players have gone yard in their first at-bat, including Hall of Fame reliever Hoyt Wilhelm, who hit the only home run of his long career the first time he stepped to the plate in 1952. But only one player has matched Nieman's feat: Cardinals catcher Keith McDonald, who homered on July 4, 2000, and again on July 6—and who was sent back to the minors on July 21.

SHOT HEARD 'RO

On October 3, 1951,

Bobby Thomson hit the most famous home run in history. But you already know that.

You may also know that on August 11 of that year, Thomson's New York Giants had trailed the Dodgers by 13 games ... that they went on a 37–7 tear to tie Brooklyn at 96–58 ... that the teams split the first two games of a three-game playoff to decide the National League championship ... that the Dodgers were leading 4-2 in the bottom of the ninth when Ralph Branca came in with two men on to face Thomson ... that at 3:58 p.m., Thomson lined a shot to leftfield that sank over the leftfield wall of the Polo Grounds ... and that Giants radio announcer Russ Hodges screamed over and over again, "The Giants win the pennant! The Giants win the pennant!"

Maybe you even know that Willie Mays was on deck when Thomson cracked his eternal blast.

So here are a few things you might not know:

1 NEW YORK CAUGHT BROOKLYN on Friday, September 28, and both teams won on Saturday. Then the Giants beat the Boston Braves, 3-2, on Sunday, forcing the Dodgers to win to make the playoff. Brooklyn trailed the NL champion Phillies 6-1 at one point, but came back to push the contest into extra innings. Jackie Robinson made a game-saving catch in the 13th, then smashed a game-winning homer off Robin Roberts in the 14th.

2 ATTENDANCE AT THE DECIDING game of the playoffs was just 34,320, as more than 20,000 seats went unfilled at the Polo Grounds—an ominous sign of things to come. The Dodgers and Giants finished no. 1 and no. 2 in National League attendance that year, but drew just 2,342,167 fans combined, down 31 percent from 1947, the last time the clubs had placed first and second in attendance. By 1951, television was sucking fans away from ballparks, just as suburbs were sucking them away from cities.

3 MONTE IRVIN is the answer to the trivia question, "Who made the last out of the 1951 season?" Irvin popped out two batters before Thomson hit his homer.

4 ENTERING THAT 157th GAME of the season, Branca had lost 11 games and given up 18 home runs in 1951. Five of the losses and 10 of the homers allowed had been against the Giants.

5 RUSS HODGES was so excited as Thomson circled the bases that he never recorded the historic home run on his scorecard, which is preserved today in the Hall of Fame.

6 AFTER THE GAME, Thomson guest-starred on Perry Como's TV show, which paid him $1,000. Then he took the Staten Island Ferry from the tip of Manhattan to Staten Island, visited the fire station where his brother worked, and walked home by himself.

7 A DECADE LATER, accusations surfaced that Thomson's home run—not to mention the Giants' end-of-season surge—was a direct consequence of stealing signs. In 1962, Thomson said the charge (made in an AP story) was "the most ridiculous thing I have ever heard of." In 2001, a *Wall Street Journal* story described how a spy in the centerfield clubhouse had relayed signals to the bench during the last three months of the 1951 season. Backup catcher Sal Yvars was quoted to the effect that, from the bullpen, he had stolen a sign intended for Branca and flashed it to Thomson. Thomson was now less adamant: "I'd have to say more no than yes. I don't like to think of something *(continued)*

taking away from it." Branca later told *The New York Times* that he'd known about the sign-stealing since 1954, but "didn't want to cheapen a legendary moment in baseball."

Did Thomson have advance warning? Not likely. Branca's first pitch was right down the middle. The second pitch—the one that became history—was up and in. Just not up enough or in enough.

Did the Giants' surge have anything to do with stealing signs at home? Not likely. They stormed back because of three things: Manager Leo Durocher moved Thomson and Whitey Lockman from the outfield to third base and first base, respectively, ensuring that Monte Irvin (no. 3 in the MVP voting that year) and a May 25 callup named Willie Mays would play regularly; Mays, after a slow start, put together a terrific rookie season; and their pitching came together in the second half—especially on the road (4.45 ERA before July 20, 3.00 after).

But even if the club was stealing signs, so what? This was baseball in the late 1940s and early 1950s. The best athletes in the world weren't yet playing basketball or football; they were on the diamond, colliding in an aggressive, physical style of play that Jackie Robinson had restored to the game. The era was marked by brushbacks, brawls, and vicious bench jockeying. And in this environment, sign-stealing—which has never been against the rules—was rampant.

Mays, watching Thomson step to the plate, realized first base was open and said later he was concerned for a moment that the Dodgers might issue an intentional walk and pitch to him instead. But they didn't.

Thomson stood in the box under enormous pressure and delivered the most game-changing, heart-stopping, world-ending home run ever.

The Giants Win the Pennant!

The Giants Win the Pennant!

The Giants Win the Pennant!

"MIRACLE OF COOGAN'S BLUFF"

by RED SMITH

New York Herald Tribune
October 4, 1951

NOW IT IS DONE. Now the story ends. And there is no way to tell it. The art of fiction is dead. Reality has strangled invention. Only the utterly impossible, the inexpressibly fantastic, can ever be plausible again.

Down on the green and white and earth-brown geometry of the playing field, a drunk tries to break through the ranks of ushers marshaled along the foul lines to keep profane feet off the diamond. The ushers thrust him back and he lunges at them, struggling in the clutch of two or three men. He breaks free, and four or five tackle him. He shakes them off, bursts through the line, runs head-on into a special park cop, who brings him down with a flying tackle.

Here comes a whole platoon of ushers. They lift him and haul him, twisting and kicking, back across the first-base line. Again he shakes loose and crashes the line. He is through. He is away, weaving out toward center field, while cheering thousands are jammed beneath the windows of the Giants' clubhouse.

At heart, our man is a Giant, too. He never gave up...

So it was the Dodgers' ball game, 4-1, and the Dodgers' pennant. So all right. Better get started and beat the crowd home. That stuff in the ninth inning? That didn't mean anything.

A single by Al Dark. A single by Don Mueller. Irvin's pop-up, Lockman's one-run double. Now the corniest possible sort of Hollywood schmaltz—stretcher-bearers plodding away with an injured Mueller between them, symbolic of the Giants themselves.

There went Newcombe and here came Ralph Branca. Who's at bat? Thomson again? He beat Branca with a home run the other day. Would Charley Dressen order him walked, putting the winning run on base, to pitch to the dead-end kids at the bottom of the batting order? No, Branca's first pitch was a called strike.

The second pitch—well, when Thomson reached first base he turned and looked toward the left-field stands. Then he started jumping straight up in the air, again and again. Then he trotted around the bases, taking his time.

Ralph Branca turned and started for the clubhouse. The number on his uniform looked huge. Thirteen.

MOST HOME RUNS
IN ALL-STAR GAMES

GAMES	PLAYERS	HR
24	Stan Musial	6
9	Fred Lynn	4
18	Ted Williams	4
5	Ralph Kiner	3
9	Rocky Colavito	3
10	Gary Carter	3
11	Harmon Killebrew	3
12	Johnny Bench	3
24	Willie Mays	3

Nine of the 19 players who took part in *Home Run Derby* eventually made it into the Hall of Fame. And 19 of the 19 had to make small talk with the earnest host, Mark Scott, who favored observations like "... a ball game's never over until the last man is out." The first show featured 50-HR men Mantle and Mays; Willie led 8-2 after five "innings," but Mickey caught him in the eighth and in the ninth crushed a ball entirely out of the park to take home his first $2,000 check. Aaron hauled in $13,500, the most of any contestant, by winning six face-offs before Wally Post outslugged him.

Sadly, Scott died of a heart attack six months after shooting the first season, so *Home Run Derby* lasted only 26 episodes (which today occasionally flicker across ESPN Classic). But the program proved fans loved to watch home runs even when the slams had nothing to do with actual games.

So did the advent of the tape-measure home run. A box score looks exactly the same whether a ball clears a fence by six inches or 60 feet. But fans love to argue about which players hit balls the hardest and whether those balls landed 400, 500, or 600 feet away from home plate. And in the 1950s, teams and sportswriters started providing numbers that purportedly answered those questions. They had to, because Mickey Mantle kept driving balls into orbit. (See the box on Mantle's tape-measure shots on page 67.)

Understand two things about Mantle's legendary blasts: He never hit a ball 643 feet, the distance the *Guinness Book of World Records* listed for his September 1960 blast in Detroit. And he probably didn't hit a ball 565 feet in Washington in 1953.

Home run distances have been exaggerated through the years because of a persistent tendency the human eye has to perceive balls as rising when they strike distant obstructions, not to mention a persistent tendency the human heart has to elevate its heroes.

Think about it this way: To get a maximal combination of distance and height, a batter has to launch a ball at something like a 45-degree angle. (At angles much greater than that, balls are popped into the air; much lower and they're driven into the ground.) Now, if you look at where batted balls strike

CONTINUED ON PAGE 84

STAN THE MAN AND THE KIDS

ON MAY 2, 1954, Stan Musial smashed three home runs in the first game of a twin bill against the Giants, then cracked two more in the nightcap. This was notable for three reasons.

1 It was the first time anybody hit five dingers in a doubleheader.

2 An 8-year-old Cardinals fan named Nate Colbert was in the stands at the old Busch Stadium that day—and he would grow up to become the only other player to homer five times in a doubleheader.

Colbert, a first baseman who was an original San Diego Padre, equaled the feat on August 1, 1972, against the Braves. At the dawn of its franchise, Colbert was San Diego's only power source: In 1972, he hit 38 of the team's 102 home runs (a percentage never matched by Barry Bonds or Mark McGwire) and drove in 111 of its 488 runs (a percentage never matched by anybody). Back trouble ruined his career after the age of 27, but for five years, Colbert was quite a slugger.

3 By the way, when Musial got home after piling up 21 total bases in the doubleheader, his 12-year-old son said to him, "Boy, that's some crummy pitching staff they've got."

66
DICK STUART
Lincoln, Western League
1956

66
SAMMY SOSA
Chicago, NL
1998

65
MARK McGWIRE
St. Louis, NL
1999

64
BOB LENNON
Nashville
Southern Association
1954

69
BOB CRUES
Amarillo
West Texas-New Mexico League
1948

69
JOE HAUSER
Minneapolis
American Association
1933

70
MARK McGWIRE
St. Louis, NL
1998

72

JOE BAUMAN, Roswell, Longhorn League, 1954

73
BARRY BONDS
San Francisco, NL
2001

Sixty HOME RUNS IN A *Season*

WHEN BARRY BONDS hit his 73rd home run in 2001, Mark McGwire wasn't the only man he knocked out of the record books. In 1954, Joe Bauman of the Roswell Rockets in the Class C Longhorn League cracked 72 homers, a pro baseball record.

Bauman was a big guy (6'5", 225 pounds) who signed with the Boston Braves but lost four seasons when her served in the navy during in World War II. In 1948, he appeared in one game for Milwaukee of the American

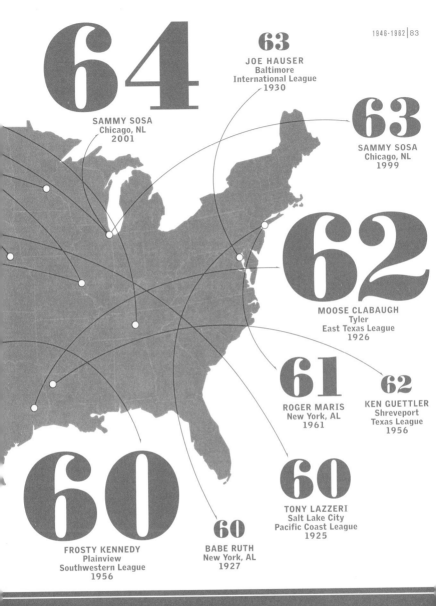

64
SAMMY SOSA
Chicago, NL
2001

63
JOE HAUSER
Baltimore
International League
1930

63
SAMMY SOSA
Chicago, NL
1999

62
MOOSE CLABAUGH
Tyler
East Texas League
1926

61
ROGER MARIS
New York, AL
1961

62
KEN GUETTLER
Shreveport
Texas League
1956

60
FROSTY KENNEDY
Plainview
Southwestern League
1956

60
BABE RUTH
New York, AL
1927

60
TONY LAZZERI
Salt Lake City
Pacific Coast League
1925

Association, the only time he got as high as Triple A. But the following season, he held out, then played semipro ball and run a gas station in Oklahoma. He returned to the minors in 1952, and in 1954, to go along with his 72 dingers, he hit .400 and drove in 224 runs. He hit 46 more homers in 1955 and retired after the 1956 season with 337 home runs and 1,057 RBI in 1,109 minor league games.

Bauman put down roots in Roswell, dying there at the age of 83 in 2005. His .916 slugging average in 1954 is still a professional record.

40 OR MORE HOME RUNS WITH 40 OR FEWER STRIKEOUTS

HR	PLAYERS	K
42	Mel Ott 1929 GIANTS	38
49	Lou Gehrig 1934 YANKEES	31
46	Joe DiMaggio 1937 YANKEES	37
40	Johnny Mize 1948 GIANTS	38
40	Ted Kluszewski 1953 REDS	34
49	Ted Kluszewski 1954 REDS	35
47	Ted Kluszewski 1955 REDS	40

"When I hit a home run I usually didn't care where it went. So long as it was a home run, that was all that mattered."

—Mickey Mantle

obstructions, in nearly all cases those points of impact make angles of less than 45 degrees with home plate. They have to, because they're much farther away from home plate than they are off the ground. So if a batted ball really was still rising when it hit such an obstruction, that would mean the hitter hadn't gotten all of the ball—he had driven it at a less than optimal angle, less than 45 degrees. And surely when he hit the ball better some other time, at a better angle, he would knock it over that obstruction.

Except at the limits of home run power, that doesn't happen. Mantle hit the Yankee Stadium rightfield facade a few times but never cleared it. The reality was, of course, that he did smash those balls at optimal angles. Which means they were already coming down when they hit the facade.

A researcher named William Jenkinson has studied the issue of long-distance home runs more thoroughly than anybody, and he makes exactly this argument. "In order for the ball to be rising at roof level, it would have to be traveling at a lower angle than that which produces maximum distance. If Mantle, or anyone else, had sufficient strength to hit a ball that was still traveling upward when it hit the towering facade, he would also have enough strength to clear the facade by a distance of at least 100 feet."

It's no insult to Mantle to point out that ridiculous numbers got attached to many of his blasts. The man hit confirmed homers of at least 450 feet to both left- and rightfield in

CONTINUED ON PAGE 89

FOUR HOME RUNS IN AN ALL-STAR GAME

JIM LEMON IS THE ONLY HITTER to have done it.

On July 19, 1955, representing the Chattanooga Lookouts in the Southern Association All-Star game, Lemon smacked four homers off the Birmingham Barons, who were in first place and faced the star players from the league's other clubs.

Lemon had bona fide power—among other feats, in 1956 he became the first Washington Senator to homer in three straight at-bats in a single game. (And he did it against Whitey Ford!) But Lemon enjoyed only a brief stay among the ranks of classic 1950s sluggers. He made it to the majors in 1950, but lost the next two seasons to the Korean War. And although he had enough speed to lead the AL in triples in 1956, and a good enough arm to lead the league in outfield double plays the same year, overall he was an awful defender: Bill James ranks Lemon the worst outfielder in history among players who had substantial careers.

Let's remember him instead as the only guy in organized baseball to smack four dingers in one All-Star game.

MOST HOME RUNS ALLOWED, *Season*

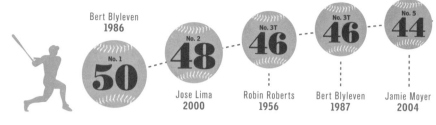

Bert Blyleven
1986

No. 1
50

No. 2
48

Jose Lima
2000

No. 3T
46

Robin Roberts
1956

No. 3T
46

Bert Blyleven
1987

No. 5
44

Jamie Moyer
2004

THE KING OF SOUVENIRS

THE LIST OF most home runs allowed in a season is full of guys who (1) exhibited extreme control, to the point where they would rather throw gopher-ball strikes than issue walks; or (2) had terrible seasons; or (3), in the cases of Jose Lima and Jamie Moyer, both.

The list of most home runs allowed in a career is full of guys who (1) had that extreme control; or (2) were around forever; or (3), in the case of Robin Roberts, both.

Roberts helped change the way baseball was played by essentially saying, "Hit as many homers off me as you can. My job is to make sure there's nobody on base when you do."

Ferguson Jenkins, who is second on the career list but who was also first or second in his league eight times in fewest walks allowed per nine innings pitched, had the same philosophy.

To a lesser extent, so did Jim Kaat, Bert Blyleven (when he pitched in the Metrodome), and Catfish Hunter (not listed, but 15th all-time in home runs surrendered).

Did any of these gopher-ball pitchers exhibit a knack for knocking balls out of parks themselves?

Thirty-one pitchers have hit 15 or more home runs in a career. (That includes Babe Ruth, who went yard 15 times as a hurler.) Of that group, only four gave up 300 or more home runs. Warren Spahn, who ranks sixth on the above list, hit 35 HR himself. Kaat, who's 10th, smacked 16. And Early Wynn gave up

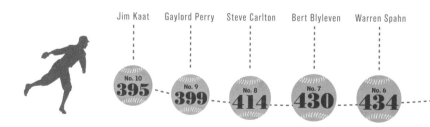

Jim Kaat

No. 10
395

Gaylord Perry

No. 9
399

Steve Carlton

No. 8
414

Bert Blyleven

No. 7
430

Warren Spahn

No. 6
434

No. 6T **43** Pedro Ramos 1957

No. 6T **43** Eric Milton 2004

No. 8 **42** Denny McLain 1966

No. 9T **41** Rick Helling 1999

No. 9T **41** Phil Niekro 1979

No. 9T **41** Robin Roberts 1955

338 homers while going yard 15 times (plus two as a pinch hitter).

And then there was Pedro Ramos.

While he wasn't in the same class as the best-hitting pitchers of all time—Wes Ferrell, Bob Lemon, Don Newcombe, Red Ruffing—he did crack 15 HR in 703 AB. But when it came to hitting and allowing home runs, he was the King of Souvenirs: 1.26 home runs either given up or hit per nine innings.

Ramos gave up a whopping 314 homers in 2,355 2/3 big-league innings. He led the AL in losses four straight years (1958 through 1961), and in home runs allowed three times. His 43 HR allowed in 1957 set a league record (subsequently broken by Blyleven). He gave up an even dozen home runs to Mickey Mantle, including a famous tape-measure blast in 1956 and an inside-the-park job in 1958.

But Ramos could play. He was a no. 1 starter, albeit for a Senators team that routinely finished low in the standings. He had tremendous speed—the Senators used him as a pinchrunner about a dozen times a year, and he challenged Mantle to a footrace to determine who was the faster. (The race never happened.)

On July 31, 1963, Woodie Held, Ramos, Tito Francona, and Larry Brown smashed consecutive homers, all off the Angels' Paul Foytack. Ramos' dinger was his second in that game.

Ramos was born in Pinar del Rio, Cuba, and in 1960 took part in the only all-Cuban triple play in major league history: The play went 1-3-6, Ramos to Julio Becquer to Jose Valdivielso. In 1963, Ramos was the losing pitcher in the first and only major league Hispanic-American All-Star game.

The definitive Pedro Ramos game came on May 12, 1961, at Minnesota. In the top of the fifth, Ramos gave up a home run to the opposing pitcher, Eli Grba of the Angels. In the bottom of the inning, he hit a home run off Grba and went on to win the game, 5-4.

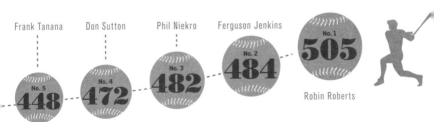

Frank Tanana

Don Sutton

Phil Niekro

Ferguson Jenkins

No. 5 **448**

No. 4 **472**

No. 3 **482**

No. 2 **484**

No. 1 **505** Robin Roberts

MOST HOME RUNS ALLOWED, *Career*

No. 1
DUKE SNIDER
326

No. 2
GIL HODGES
310

No. 3
EDDIE MATHEWS
299

No. 4
MICKEY MANTLE
280

No. 5
STAN MUSIAL
266

No. 6
YOGI BERRA
256

No. 7
WILLIE MAYS
250

No. 8
TED KLUSZEWSKI
239

No. 9
GUS ZERNIAL
232

No. 10
ERNIE BANKS
228

MOST HOME RUNS

1950 1959

every ballpark in the American League. It's just that reports of tape-measure shots before 1982, when MLB teams began using a computer system to calculate distances, need to be taken with a huge grain of salt ... and Mantle hit more of them than anyone.

And you know what? Those home runs won a truckload of games. The Yankees' power was disguised somewhat by their stadium, but thanks to Mantle, it was their core strength in an era they thoroughly dominated: The club led the AL in road home runs nine times from 1951 to 1962.

THE HOMER VS. THE SHIFT

A HOME RUN ONCE beat the "Williams Shift," a defensive tactic in which infielders would cluster on the right side of second base (and out into short right) and dare Ted Williams to punch the ball the opposite way. The Splendid Splinter, as obstinate as he was gifted, rarely took the dare.

But on September 13, 1946, facing the Indians (whose player-manager, Lou Boudreau, had popularized the shift), Williams—whether by design or bad timing was never made clear—drove a ball to left-center field that rolled to the fence. Williams ran all the way around the bases, sliding into the plate for the only inside-the-park home run of his career. The Red Sox won, 1-0, and clinched the American League pennant.

After the game, Williams—who always referred to the defensive ploy as the "Boudreau Shift"—was asked if it had been the easiest homer he ever hit.

"Hell, no," he said. "It was the hardest. I had to run."

Mantle walked so often that he scored more runs than he drove in and had a batch of seasons with relatively few at-bats. But look closely at his lines in and around 1956 (his Triple Crown season) and 1961 (the chase with Maris). Like 1954, when he led the league in runs scored with 129. Or 1955, when he led the league in homers, triples and walks. Or 1958, or 1962 ...

Yet during Mantle's most productive years, many sportswriters harped on his strikeouts, sometimes blaming his power for warping his approach to hitting. When he retired, they focused on the fact that his lifetime batting average had sunk under .300. In 1972, for instance, the longtime

CHARLIE MAXWELL, TIGERS	1960	5
WILLIE MAYS, GIANTS	1955	4
RON GANT, REDS	1995	4
MARK McGWIRE, CARDINALS	1998	4
CHIPPER JONES, BRAVES	1999	4
JIM THOME, INDIANS	2001	4

MOST EXTRA-INNING HOME RUNS, SEASON

CHARLIE MAXWELL was nicknamed Paw Paw and Smokey, but was best known as the Sunday Home Run Hitter. Of his 148 career homers, he hit 40 on Sunday, and 12 of those came against the Yankees. Maxwell himself traced his celebrity to a Sunday doubleheader the Tigers swept from New York on May 3, 1959. Entering the first game batting .182, he went two for four with a home run in the ninth inning, then blasted three homers in his first three at-bats in the second game.

Maxwell spent nearly 800 games in the minors and was through as a big-leaguer by the age of 37, but in between he had an outstanding five-year run. He hit around .270 with power, drew 70 walks a season, and used to catch shagged fly balls behind his back.

GREATEST FORGOTTEN
HOME RUNS

WHEN TWO BIG, similar events occur in close proximity, the more recent often winds up overshadowing the earlier one. Case in point: Frank Robinson won the Triple Crown in 1966 and Carl Yastrzemski won it in 1967 with equally devastating seasons. But many more fans remember Yaz's year, partly because he carried the Red Sox to their "Impossible Dream" pennant, but mostly because his Triple Crown came right after Robinson's and nobody has won one since.

So it is with a pair of the most dramatic home runs of all time.

In 1950, the Phillies, after a squandering a 7 1/2-game lead in the preceding two weeks, still had a one-game lead when they squared off against the second-place Dodgers in the final game of the regular season. A Dodgers win would force a playoff. With Robin Roberts and Don Newcombe on the mound, the score was 1-1 after nine innings. Roberts led off the 10th with a single. After a single and a failed bunt, Dick Sisler stepped to the plate.

A left-handed hitter who already had three hits, Sisler was playing with a sprained right wrist. He was also playing with a rose in his pocket. On the way to the ballpark, the taxicab carrying Sisler, Del Ennis, Russ Meyer, and Willie "Puddin' Head" Jones and a car carrying a priest were stopped at a traffic light. The priest recognized the players and offered Sisler a flower.

"Father, I'm not Catholic," Sisler said.

"Take it anyway," the priest replied. "Maybe it will bring you good luck." (And maybe the priest was a Giants fan.)

Sisler, his wrist heavily taped, clouted Newcombe's fourth pitch over the leftfield wall. After Roberts put down the Dodgers in the bottom of the inning, Philadelphia had its first pennant since 1915.

Great story, great game, topped by a blast that deserves to be legendary. But just a year later, Bobby Thomson hit an even more amazing shot to cap an even more amazing pennant race.

A decade after Sisler's now-all-but-forgotten blast, the Yankees and the Pirates scrapped their way to Game 7 of one of the craziest World Series ever. The three Pirates wins had come in tight contests: 6-4, 3-2, 5-2. The three Bombers wins had been routs: a combined score of 38-3.

In Game 7 in Forbes Field, the Pirates went up 2-0 when Rocky Nelson homered in the first. The Bucs then scored two more runs in the second. But Moose Skowron went deep in the fifth, Yogi Berra cracked a three-run dinger in the sixth, and the Yankees picked up two more runs in the eighth. By the time the Pirates got down to their final six outs, they were trailing, 7-4.

The Pirates clawed back in the eighth, scoring two runs. Then, with two outs, two men on base, and two strikes, reserve catcher Hal Smith smashed a home run over the leftfield wall, giving the Pirates a two-run lead and sending the crowd of 36,683 into delirium.

"Forbes Field is an outdoor insane asylum!" exclaimed NBC radio announcer Chuck Thompson. "We have seen and shared in one of baseball's great moments!"

Absolutely true. Smith's blast was one of the greatest home runs in World Series history. But his moment in the sun was briefer even than Sisler's. In the top of the ninth, the Yankees tied the game. And in the bottom of the ninth, Bill Mazeroski hit the greatest home run in World Series history.

8
Andy Prevedello (CF)

7
Don Pulford (SS)   Luis Torres (2B)   **9**

Ron Wilkins (LF)   **6**   **4**   Fred Fillipelli (RF)

Darrel McCall (3B)   Frank Van Burkleo (1B)

5   **3**

Bob Clear (P)
1

Rich Binford (C)
2

9 1 9

PLAYERS   LINEUP   HOMERS

ONLY ONCE in the history of organized baseball has every member of a starting lineup cracked a home run in the same game. It happened for the Douglas Copper Kings on August 19, 1958, in a game against the Chihuahua Dorados in the Class C Arizona-Mexico League. None of the nine Copper Kings ever made it to the majors, so here's their chance to be remembered: Don Pulford, SS; Andy Prevedello, CF; Ron Wilkins, LF; Frank Van Burkleo, 1B; Luis Torres, 2B; Fred Fillipelli, RF; Darrel McCall, 3B; Rich Binford, C; Bob Clear, P. Clear was the manager as well as the starting pitcher. Wilkins went six for six. The Copper Kings won, 22-8, in a game called on account of darkness after eight innings.

(and usually astute) *New York Times* columnist Arthur Daley wrote in his book *All the Home Run Kings*, "The Oklahoma Kid failed to achieve the consistency that marked the careers of the superstars."

Even stories about Mantle's courage in playing through painful injuries are tinged with regret for what he didn't do, rather than appreciation for what he did. A typical quote, from Nellie Fox: "On two legs, Mickey Mantle would have been the greatest ballplayer who ever lived." Well, okay, but he came pretty close to being the greatest on however many legs he had. It's as if Mantle's 536 home runs, the products of his central skill, are hidden in plain sight when it comes to evaluating his career.

The truth is that Mantle's power put a huge number of runs on the scoreboard. He scored 1,677 runs and drove in 1,509 over his career, while making 5,899 outs. That means he was generating 7.3 runs per 27 outs, while the average AL team was scoring just 4.3 runs per game.

Ruth's Yankees made it to seven World Series and DiMaggio's to 10. But Mantle carried his team to 12—in the post-integration era and with fewer Hall of Famers to help. And all the while, he ran the bases with his head down after hitting a home run. He explained, "I figured the pitcher already felt bad enough without me showing him up."

THE MEN WHO HIT home runs by the bucketfuls tend to define their teams, for better or worse. With Rocky Colavito, it was all for the better.

Rocco Domenico Colavito grew up in the Bronx, about a mile away from Yankee Stadium, in the Joe DiMaggio era. He signed with the Cleveland Indians as a pitcher-outfielder at the age of 17, led the Eastern League in homers and RBI two years later, and led the American Association with 38 dingers in 1954.

At that point, based on his minor league numbers, he was ready for the Show. But the Indians had just won 111 games, they had brought Ralph Kiner over from the Cubs, and manager Al Lopez wasn't sold on Colavito, so Rocky went back to Indianapolis. But Colavito had an ally in another Bronx-born slugger—Indians GM Hank Greenberg. After Rocky started the 1956 season by hitting 12 homers in his first 35 games for San Diego in the Pacific Coast League, Greenberg got Lopez to bring him up. Colavito cracked Cleveland's lineup for good on July 26, 1956, and went on to clout 21 HR in 322 at-bats.

And so a lakefront legend was born.

The 6'3", 190-pound Colavito had immense power and a rifle arm. He also had dark, soft, movie-star good looks and a cheerful personality. In Cleveland he became not just a home run champion, but a matinee idol, tireless autograph signer, and all-around fan favorite. "He loves everyone," said Greenberg, "and everyone loves him."

Frank Lane, who succeeded Greenberg and was as unsentimental as any GM who has ever plied the trade, sneeringly called Colavito "Salesman Sam," but stopped when he realized the young slugger was sincere. Colavito genuinely basked in—and returned—the Cleveland fans' affection. Cleveland sportswriter Hal

Lebovitz once wrote, "Don't knock the Rock," and the phrase became the title of Colavito's biography.

Colavito had a distinctive style at the plate. He would place his bat behind his back across his shoulder blades, then twist his upper body back and forth and bend up and down to loosen his shoulders before stepping into the box. It worked. In 1958, he had a monster season, smashing 41 homers and leading the AL in slugging percentage, while posting an on-base average over .400. The following year, he led the league with 42 dingers and his blasts started getting national attention; *The Sporting News* wrote that Colavito was the slugger most likely to break Babe Ruth's single-season home run record.

On June 10, 1959, Colavito became the eighth player to hit four home runs in a game, going deep in four straight at-bats in an 11-8 win at Baltimore. Rocky was excited as he crossed home plate after his fourth tater, but Cleveland manager Joe Gordon and the other Indians seemed stunned. Rightly so: Before Colavito hit four by himself, no team had hit four homers in one game at Memorial Stadium since the Orioles started playing there in 1954. At their next Sunday home game, the Indians sold 21,000 walk-up tickets. Overall attendance more than doubled that year.

Then the unthinkable happened: 48 hours before Opening Day, 1960, Lane traded Colavito to the Tigers for Harvey Kuenn, who had just led the AL with a .353 batting average. Lane was wary of the leverage the popular Colavito was building—Rocky had briefly held out that spring—and he probably just couldn't resist the sheer notoriety of trading a home-run king for a batting champion.

Aside from the emotional attachment, Indians fans had plenty of reasons to blast the deal. Colavito had a massive power advantage; he had just hit more home runs in one year than Kuenn had in his best four combined. Plus

ROCKY COLAVITO

ROCKY COLAVITO STATS

Year	Team	G	R	HR	RBI	BB	AVG	OPS
1955	Indians	5	3	0	0	0	.444	1.111
1956	Indians	101	55	21	65	49	.276	.903
1957	Indians	134	66	25	84	71	.252	.819
1958	Indians	143	80	41	113	84	.303	1.024
1959	Indians	154	90	42	111	71	.257	.849
1960	Tigers	145	67	35	87	53	.249	.791
1961	Tigers	163	129	45	140	113	.290	.982
1962	Tigers	161	90	37	112	96	.273	.885
1963	Tigers	160	91	22	91	84	.271	.795
1964	Athletics	160	89	34	102	83	.274	.873
1965	Indians	162	92	26	108	93	.287	.851
1966	Indians	151	68	30	72	76	.238	.767
1967	Indians/White Sox	123	30	8	50	49	.231	.651
1968	Dodgers/Yankees	79	21	8	24	29	.211	.683
	Career Totals	1841	971	374	1159	951	.266	.848

Rocky got on base just as often as the man he was traded for: At the time of the trade, Colavito's career OBP was .364, while Kuenn's was .360. Colavito was only 26, while Kuenn was 29. It was, in short, the worst trade in Indians history.

Without Colavito, Cleveland in 1960 dropped from first in the AL in home runs to fourth and from first in the league in runs scored to fifth. Attendance plunged 37 percent. Kuenn lasted one season with the Indians before Lane traded him, too. It would be 34 years before the team finished above third place again, leading Terry Pluto to write a wonderful history of the franchise called *The Curse of Rocky Colavito*.

Meanwhile, after a bumpy start in Detroit—Al Kaline was The Man fans worshipped there—the Rock kept blasting away. He cracked 139 homers in four years with the Tigers, even keeping pace with Roger Maris and Mickey Mantle in the early going en route to a 45-HR, 140-RBI season in 1961. Before the 1964 season, Colavito was dealt to Kansas City, where he put up typical numbers: .274, 34 homers, 102 RBI, 83 walks.

And then the flailing Indians, in what might be the second-worst trade in team history, gave up Tommy John (age 21) and Tommie Agee (22) to get the now-31-year-old Colavito back. Rocky led the AL in RBIs and walks in 1965, but his skills were fading. He cracked 30 homers in 1966 but batted just .238, and after that season, his power plunged as well.

Colavito's relationship with Indians fans, though, was still love since first sight. From 1964 through 1967, Cleveland's attendance totals were 653,293, 934,786, 903,359, and 662,980. Can you guess which two of those years the Rock patrolled the outfield exclusively for the Tribe?

Colavito's last magical moment came on August 25, 1968. By then he was playing for his hometown Yankees. With the team trailing Detroit 5-0 in the first game of a doubleheader, Rocky came in to pitch for only the second time in his big-league career. He got Kaline and Willie Horton out and pitched 2 2/3 scoreless innings while New York rallied to win, thereby picking up a W—the last position player to do so until 2000.

HANK AARON

CHAPTER 4

1963-1976

Counterpunch

Armchair historians love to overanalyze the 1960s, and armchair baseball historians are no exception. My favorite example is the 2003 book *The Single-Season Home Run Kings*, in which William F. McNeil presents chapters on Babe Ruth, Roger Maris, Mark McGwire, and Barry Bonds. Connecting them is another chapter called "The 1960s to the 1990s—An Historical Perspective." His analysis:

"The United States

became embroiled in another land confrontation, this one in Vietnam," McNeil writes. "Thousands of other young people, children of the Baby Boomer generation, 'dropped out' of society, living in communes, falling under the influence of drugs ... practicing free sex ... Expansion continued unabated."

The real-world events of that era and the history of home runs *were* related, but as they almost always are: not so much by cause and effect, but by having a common ancestor. The massive demographic shifts that followed World War II ultimately gave us the baseball of the 1960s and early '70s as well as McNeil's free sex. In 1962, one year after Roger Maris and Mickey Mantle raced to break Ruth's single-season record, major leaguers bashed a record 3,001 dingers. And then the bottom fell out. Homers dropped 10 percent in 1963 and kept falling ... and falling.

What happened?

People had moved, and teams had followed. Following the stasis of the early 1950s, franchises finally started to catch up with the waves of Americans who were leaving Rust Belt cities. The Braves, Dodgers, Giants, Athletics, and Senators all headed west, but even many of the teams that didn't bolt their metropolitan areas did relocate from hemmed-in downtowns to shiny new suburban stadiums. Today, Shea Stadium in Queens is best known as a place with terrible bathrooms, or maybe for being surrounded by auto-body chop shops. But 40 years ago, it was a glittering, state-of-the-art facility that promised to lure New York families who had fled to Long Island back to baseball.

And nearly every one of the new stadiums built during this great migration turned homers into singles or outs. Freed from the cozy confines of urban neighborhoods, teams began build-

1964

THE ASSOCIATED PRESS expanded boxscores to include season-to-date totals for players who homered, listing them in parentheses below game lineups.

No. 1
HARMON KILLEBREW
393

No. 2
HANK AARON
375

No. 3
WILLIE MAYS
350

No. 4
RANK ROBINSON
316

No. 5
WILLIE McCOVEY
300

No. 6
FRANK HOWARD
288

No. 7
NORM CASH
278

No. 8
ERNIE BANKS
269

No. 9
MICKEY MANTLE
256

No. 10
ORLANDO CEPEDA
254

MOST HOME RUNS
1960 **1969**

BEST FANTASY WEEK EVER

FROM SUNDAY, MAY 12, through Saturday, May 18, 1968, Frank Howard blasted 10 homers, the most by any player in a calendar week. Despite Howard's heroics, the Washington Senators, who were destined to finish 10th that season, lost three of the six games they played that week. Why? Because they couldn't get on base; Hondo's dingers were all solo shots.

ing big parks with lots of seats and lots of foul-ball territory, and kept building them for 20 or so years. Municipal governments helped the trend along by being willing to fund stadiums as long as they served as multi-purpose arenas, meaning as long as they were big enough for football, too.

Sportsman's Park, home to the St. Louis Browns, had been a great hitter's field: In 1922, Ken Williams hit 32 homers with 103 RBI there, and 7 HR and 52 RBI on the road. In 1954, the Browns moved to Memorial Stadium in Baltimore, became the Orioles, and promptly hit a grand total of 52 homers, 36 percent fewer than any other team in the American League. The Giants ended up in Candlestick Park and the Dodgers in Dodger Stadium, nasty parks for hitters. The Mets moved from the Polo Grounds, with its 258-foot rightfield line, to Shea, with its awful visibility. The Astrodome opened in 1965. In May 1966, the Cardinals moved from the former Sportsman's Park, where the Cards and their opponents hit a total of 171 HR in 1965, to Busch Stadium, where they hit 107 in 1967. In June 1970, the Reds relocated from Crosley Field (171 HR in 1969) to Riverfront Stadium (120 HR in 1971).

It all seems obvious—and it is—but most of us still don't adjust for ballpark effects. Raw numbers and boxscores are what brand our brains, leaving the lasting impression, for example, that the Dodgers of the mid-1960s were a bunch of Punch-and-Judy hitters dragged to the World Series by two great pitchers. In reality, that team played under conditions like Coors Field in reverse. Even most serious fans still believe Hank Aaron was a steady hitter capable of clocking in at about 40 homers a year, not the threat to Maris he would have been had he played someplace other than County Stadium in Milwaukee.

Other factors contributed to the second coming of deadball. On January 26, 1963, baseball's Rules Committee expanded the strike zone. It had extended from the top of the batter's knees to his armpits; now it would reach from the bottom of his knees to his shoulders. At the time, it seemed like a minor change, and certainly the committee intended it as such, but strikeouts immediately soared by more than 1,200. Regular cross-country travel, which became common as teams dispersed, probably hurt the first generation of hitters to experience jet lag, too.

Then, too, by the end of the 1960s, the once-in-a-lifetime infusion of talent provided by integration was running out of steam, as

BEST HOME RUN SONG

LIKE ALL GREAT NOVELTY HITS, the best home run songs start with a listenable genre, add a wacky surprise, and create a combination you can't get out of your head. In 1970, Sam (Moore) and Dave (Prater) weren't on speaking terms, but they got together with Atlantic Records' house band, the Dixie Flyers (who also sang backup for Aretha Franklin), to record "Knock It Out the Park." This soul four-bagger, complete with batted ball sound effects, related advice from Sister Jones that's downright sabermetric:

When - you swing   swing for the___ fences

Hitting in - a   double play___   just don't make no sense.

Even better, after Hank Aaron broke Babe Ruth's lifetime home run record in 1974, Willie Dixon invited his buddy McKinley Mitchell to sing lead on a tribute called "That Last Home Run." With Mitchell roaring—"Hank was going strong when he hit that last home run"—and Dixon's Chicago Blues All-Stars rolling, the result was amazing and appropriate: Chicago blues transformed into triumph.

No. 1
WILLIE STARGELL
296

No. 2
REGGIE JACKSON
292

No. 3
JOHNNY BENCH
290

No. 4
BOBBY BONDS
280

No. 5
LEE MAY
270

No. 6T
DAVE KINGMAN
252

No. 6T
GRAIG NETTLES
252

No. 8
MIKE SCHMIDT
235

No. 9
TONY PEREZ
226

No. 10
REGGIE SMITH
225

MOST HOME RUNS

1970 1979

the best of the black and Latin American power hitters who followed Jackie Robinson started winding down their careers.

Despite all the conditions working to keep balls in the park, the list of hitters who blasted the most home runs in the 1960s is probably the most impressive of any decade, and includes Aaron, Willie Mays, Willie McCovey, and Ernie Banks; Orlando Cepeda's at no. 10. For a variety of reasons—no more Negro Leagues waiting to be tapped, increasing opportunities in other sports for black athletes, random chance—the players who replaced them weren't quite as great.

As home runs kept dropping—to a total of 2,743 in 1966, 2,299 in 1967, and just 1,995 in 1968, "the Year of the Pitcher"—batting averages and runs scored fell too. And here's something else most of us don't fully get yet: That meant homers were more valuable, even at the cost of dramatically increased strikeouts.

Modern power hitters like Harmon Killebrew have suffered in historical evaluations because they whiffed so often. But think about it: When games are being decided by 2-1 scores instead of 9-7, every run is worth more. And when no team is able to score consistently by stringing together three hits be-cause the league is hitting .247, singles and doubles are worth less. With two strikes, Joe DiMaggio could aim for a hit rather than a home run. Guys ahead of him were probably on base, and guys behind him would drive him in—and if they didn't in a given inning, they probably would next time around. But Reggie Jackson helped his team more by swinging for the fences.

The fans noticed all this and, despite the new parks, re-sponded by staying home: National League attendance plunged 23 percent from 1966 to 1968. After the 1968 season, in which only seven players hit 30 or more homers, baseball took its first

MOST HOME RUNS HIT AS A TEENAGER

1.	Tony Conigliaro	24
2.	Mel Ott	19
3.	Ken Griffey Jr.	16
4.	Phil Cavarretta	14
5.	Mickey Mantle	13
6.	Ed Kranepool	12
7.	Robin Yount	11
8.	Harmon Killebrew	8
9T.	Cesar Cedeno	7
9T.	Jimmy Sheckard	7

This is the only list where Ed Kranepool, whose name is the password to most of my accounts, could possibly share room with Mickey Mantle. So it had to go in.

major steps since 1930 to help hitters. The pitcher's mound was lowered from a height of 15 inches to 10 inches for the 1969 season. As important as that calibration was MLB's statement that officials would be enforcing the new height, because to help their power pitchers, several teams had let their mounds grow beyond 15 inches. And the strike zone was shortened again, to extend from a batter's armpits to the top of his knees. Meanwhile, the Athletics, Braves, Dodgers, Phillies, and White Sox all moved their fences in.

These changes, along with another round of expansion, pumped up homers in 1969. And four years later, the American League added the designated hitter, which helped boost home runs by 377 and attendance by almost 2 million. (Tony Oliva hit the first home run by a DH, on April 6, 1973.)

But it would take a while for teams to adjust the strategies they had developed during the years when runs where so hard to come by, and for players to shake off the effects of Deadball II. As late as 1976, five teams hit 66 or fewer home runs for the entire season.

So sluggers from this generation wound up with depressed stats. This era produced a group of mashers who had frightening power

"It would have been a helluva lot more fun if I had not hit those 61 home runs."

-Roger Maris

but whose numbers would have looked better had they played at nearly any other time: Dick Allen, Frank Howard, Jimmy Wynn. It also featured a number of power hitters who ought to rank with the all-time greats at their positions, but who don't get mentioned on many lists because their raw homer totals and batting averages were kept down: Sal Bando, Bill Freehan, Graig Nettles. In the context of its time and place, Frank Robinson's 1967 season of 30 HR and 94 RBI was every bit as valuable as Mark McGwire's 65 HR and 147 RBI in 1999. Whether fans will come to recognize it as such now that the offensive explosion of the late 1990s seems to be over is an open question.

The second half of the second deadball era came to be known for a quest. It was a pursuit of a record by a man who was actually helped by park effects as his career advanced, who maintained his ability to hit for average and get on base while focusing on slugging, whose career started in the Negro Leagues but who played strong right through the mid-1970s. That man was, of course, Hank Aaron.

In 1952, Dewey Griggs, a Braves scout, saw Aaron (then a 17-year-old shortstop) play a doubleheader for the Indianapolis Clowns.

CONTINUED ON PAGE 109

> ## "I didn't have evil intentions, but I guess I did have power."
> —Harmon Killebrew

MOST HOME RUNS IN A SINGLE SEASON,
BY POSITION

LINE-UP CARD

69 *

1998
Cardinals

2002
Rangers

57

1B	A	Mark McGwire	R
	B		
2B	A	Rogers Hornsby	R
	B	Davey Johnson	R
SS	A	Alex Rodriguez	R
	B		
3B	A	Mike Schmidt	R
	B	Adrian Beltre	L
OF	A	Barry Bonds	
	B		R
C	A	Javy Lopez	
	B		L
DH	A	David Ortiz	
	B		R
P	A	Wes Ferrell	
	B		
	A		

42

1922 Cardinals
1973 Braves

In 1973, Davey Johnson hit 42 homers as a second baseman for Atlanta (43 overall), tying Rogers Hornsby for the single-season HR record for the position. Darrell Evans added 41 and Hank Aaron hit his 40th on the next to last day of the season, making the 1976–1985 Braves the first team to have three hitters with 40 or more home runs in one year. Said Evans, "Davey and I knew that the only way we would be in the Hall of Fame was if we all hit 40 homers."

48

1980 Phillies
2004 Dodgers

2001 San Francisco Giants

42*

2003 Braves

71*

43

2005 Red Sox

9 **1931** Indians

* Don't forget interleague play and the DH.

MOST PINCH-HIT HOME RUNS, CAREER

1. Cliff Johnson — **20**
2. Jerry Lynch — **18**
3T. Gates Brown — **16**
3T. Smoky Burgess — **16**
3T. Willie McCovey — **16**
6. George Crowe — **14**
7T. Joe Adcock — **12**
7T. Bob Cerv — **12**
7T. Jose Morales — **12**
7T. Graig Nettles — **12**

"IN HIGH SCHOOL," Gates Brown once said, "I took a little English, some science, some hubcaps, and some wheel covers." But after a 1958–1959 stint at the Ohio State Reformatory, Brown straightened out his life, signed with the Tigers, hit the big leagues in 1963, and became one of Detroit's most popular players for a dozen seasons. In a sign of things to come, he hit a pinch home run in his first major-league at bat on June 19, 1963.

The Tigers of the 1960s had a surplus of All-Star-caliber players across the outfield at at first base—in 1968, manager Mayo Smith famously played centerfielder Mickey Stanley at shortstop in the World Series to get Al Kaline into the lineup—and Brown was never able to crack their starting lineup for a full season. Instead, he became a pinch-hitting specialist, and in 1968, he put up one of the all-time great off-the-bench contributions to a pennant-winning team: 18 pinch hits in 39 at-bats, for a .462 average.

Brown, who never learned why his mother nicknamed him "Gates," was listed generously at 5'11" and 220 pounds. Spending most of his time on the bench certainly gave him plenty of opportunities to munch during games. In one 1968 game, he had readied a couple of hot dogs just as he was called on to pinch hit. He stuffed the dogs into his jersey, cracked a double into the gap, slid into second base, and came up smeared with mustard and ketchup.

But the man could hit. That same month, he beat the Red Sox with a pinch home run in the 14th inning of the first game of a doubleheader, then singled home the winning run in the ninth inning of the nightcap.

Aaron went seven for nine with one homer, but between the games, Griggs inquired about Aaron's seemingly unimpressive arm. "Can't you throw any harder than that?" the scout asked.

"Sure I can," Aaron replied. "I only throw hard enough to get the runner out."

Nearly two decades later, Aaron, by then a superstar and a veteran, tutored young Braves Dusty Baker and Ralph Garr on how to pace themselves during the long big-league season. "Now, you got to play 150 games a year," he told them, "so pick your spots. You can miss just two games a month. So pick the days you're gonna be hurt, or you're gonna rest, or you're gonna have a drink or two. The rest of the time, be out on that field."

MOST AT-BATS WITHOUT A HR, SEASON

WHAT DOES IT TAKE to make it through a full major-league season without hitting any home runs? Ideally, you would be great in the field, or at least look great, so people wouldn't mind so much what you did with the bat. You would have speed and play in a ballpark that favors speed, to compensate for your lack of power. And you would play in an era of specialization, when all players aren't supposed to have the same skills.

In other words, you would be a 1960s–1970s shortstop.

With homers and batting averages down and turf fields presenting new challenges, managers throughout this era decided they could sacrifice power for speed. Homers are worth more in low-scoring eras—every run is more valuable—but are harder to find. And for the top and bottom of their lineups, teams started looking to players who could turn singles into doubles on offense and doubles into singles on defense.

Result: Baseball left behind the 1950s and created a *modus operandi* that the *Moneyball* generation would later rail against.

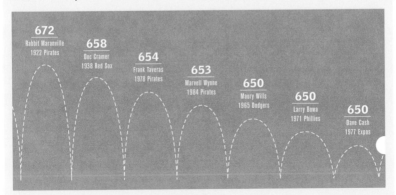

672 Rabbit Maranville 1922 Pirates

658 Doc Cramer 1938 Red Sox

654 Frank Taveras 1978 Pirates

653 Marvell Wynne 1984 Pirates

650 Maury Wills 1965 Dodgers

650 Larry Bowa 1971 Phillies

650 Dave Cash 1977 Expos

Both stories are Aaron through and through. He converted immense talent into results with maximum efficiency. That's a skill that's not merely useful—it's central to greatness in baseball. Cheap sportswriting and cheap sentiment favor violent cliches, the all-or-nothing player, the moment of maximum impact. But there was nothing violent about Henry Aaron.

Stories written early in Aaron's career often called him indolent or sleepy. Later, comments he made, such as protesting living conditions for black members of the Braves during spring training in Florida in 1961 or calling for a moment of silence to honor Martin Luther King Jr. in 1974, triggered as much surprise as controversy. Fans were shocked again when he said recently that he has kept many of the thousands of pieces of hate mail he got while pursuing the career home-run record. People have been mistaking Aaron's calm determination for the quiet of a simple man his whole career.

But it was Aaron's purposefulness that enabled him to break Ruth's record instead of being broken by the chase. It's hard now to understand the pressure he was under in 1973 and 1974, as celebrity media culture had started to grow out of control but athletes weren't yet able to wall themselves off from the outside world. Aaron got thousands of letters during his pursuit of Ruth's record, many insanely hateful. Fans, writers, photographers, and tour buses, not to mention death threats, followed him everywhere.

So did the fact that he was a black man laying siege to white America's most cherished sports record. Aaron once said, "I have never lived a day in my life that in some way—some small way, somewhere—someone didn't remind me that I'm black."

And as he approached Ruth, reminders were continually thrust in his face. During the 1973-74 offseason, Aaron appeared on the *Dean Martin Celebrity Roast.* On the show, Rat Pack member Joey Bishop recommended that when Aaron passed Ruth, he circle the bases, drop his pants, and sing "Black Bottom."

Aaron took it all in stride. Pressure didn't destroy his health, the way it did Jackie Robinson's. Injustice didn't lead him to play angry, the way it did Frank Robinson. He responded to both by redoubling his resolve.

"Baseball is a game of the long season, of relentless and gradual averaging out," John Updike has written. "Irrelevance—since the reference point of most individual games is

CONTINUED ON PAGE 115

MAY 14, 1978

After Cubs slugger Dave Kingman hit three home runs on a 10-7, 15-inning victory by Chicago over Los Angeles, Paul Olden of the Associated Press asked Tommy Lasorda, Dodgers manager ...

Olden:

What's your opinion of Kingman's performance?

Lasorda: **What's my opinion of Kingman's performance? What the *[BLEEP]* do you think is my opinion of it? I think it was *[BLEEP]*ing *[BLEEP]*. Put that in, I don't give a *[BLEEP]*. Opinion of his performance? *[BLEEP]*, he beat us with three *[BLEEP]*ing home runs! What the *[BLEEP]*do you mean, "What is my opinion of his performance?" How could you ask me a question like that, "What is my opinion of his performance?" *[BLEEP]*, he hit three home runs! *[BLEEP]*. I'm *[BLEEP]*ing pissed off to lose that *[BLEEP]*ing game. And you ask me my opinion of his performance! *[BLEEP]*. That's a tough question to ask me, isn't it? "What is my opinion of his performance?"**

Olden: **Yes, it is. I asked it, and you gave me an answer...**

Lasorda: **That's a tough question to ask me right now, "What is my opinion of his performance?" I mean, you want me to tell you what my opinion of his performance is.**

Olden: **You just did.**

Lasorda: **That's right. *[BLEEP]*. Guy hits three home runs against us. *[BLEEP]*.**

HOME & ROAD: *Hank Aaron*

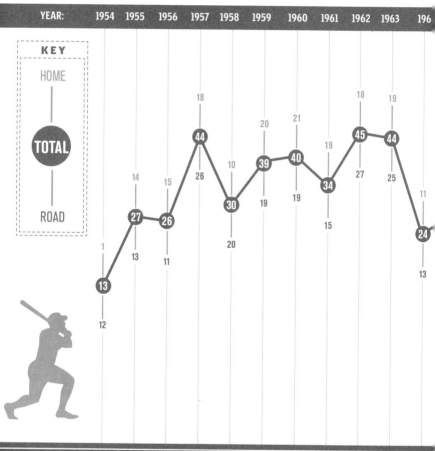

KEY

HOME

TOTAL

ROAD

HANK AARON IS OFTEN SEEN as a paragon of consistency, not only because of his level personality, but also because of his statistics. The Home Run King's yearly totals, after all, show him to be a hitter who pumped out excellent seasons like clockwork, but lacked historically explosive power. He had eight 40-plus HR campaigns but never hit 50 in a season. But this is largely an illusion created by where he played.

As Bill James pointed out the first edition of his *Historical Baseball Abstract*, Aaron played the first part of his career in Milwaukee County Stadium, a terrible HR park that was never regarded as such because the Braves of his era had such fearsome sluggers that they posted outstanding HR totals anyway. In 1957, when Aaron hit 44

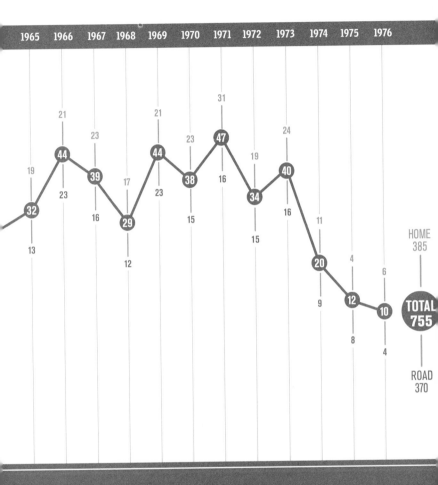

| 1965 | 1966 | 1967 | 1968 | 1969 | 1970 | 1971 | 1972 | 1973 | 1974 | 1975 | 1976 |

HOME
385

TOTAL
755

ROAD
370

HR and was the NL MVP, the Braves hit 75 HR at home but a whopping 124 on the road. During his years in Milwaukee, Aaron hit a total of 195 HR at home and 225 away.

But when the Braves moved to Atlanta in 1966, Aaron started to enjoy a reverse effect from playing in Atlanta-Fulton County Stadium. During his years in Atlanta, Aaron socked 190 HR at home and 145 on the road.

Aaron's early numbers masked power that would have netted him 50 to 60 HR a year at his peak in a typical ballpark. His later stats obscured his decline due to age —and gave his career totals a late-stage kick that made his overall record tough for other hitters to approach until recently. Being "ahead of Aaron's pace" doesn't mean much, because, helped by his home field, Aaron began a five-year HR binge at the age of 35.

MOST EXTRA-INNING HOME RUNS, CAREER

22 No. 1 **WILLIE MAYS**

18 No. 2 **JACK CLARK**

16 No. 3 **FRANK ROBINSON / BABE RUTH**

14 No. 4 **HANK AARON / JIMMIE FOXX / MICKEY MANTLE**

13 No. 5 **TED WILLIAMS**

12 No. 6 **MARK McGWIRE / RAFAEL PALMEIRO / WILLIE STARGELL**

FOR ALL HIS POWER and speed and flair, and for all the spectacular plays he made in center field, Willie Mays isn't widely remembered for many specific, "historic" home runs

Even Mays himself claims he hit only one "dramatic-type" homer in his career. It came on September 15, 1965, in the Astrodome. The Giants were leading a tight pennant race, but they trailed Houston 5-3 with two outs in the ninth inning. With Jesus Alou on first, Astros reliever Claude Raymond threw Mays 13 straight fastballs—and Mays fouled each one off. On the 14th pitch, Mays looked fooled, but he recovered—"Willie bailed out," Raymond said, "but opened up on the ball at the same time, the way only he could"—and knocked the ball over the left-centerfield wall. The Giants won the game in the 10th, but lost the pennant race to the Dodgers.

Say, hey, Willie, that's not the only big-drama dinger you hit. How about that game with the Braves on July 3, 1963, when Warren Spahn and Juan Marichal hooked up in one of the greatest pitchers' duels of all time? Neither one gave up a run through 15 innings. Marichal got through the top of the 16th, too, and then Mays homered off Spahn in the bottom of the 16th to win the game, 1-0.

Think about it. A guy leads the world in extra-inning home runs, with 20 percent more than the next guy, you figure at least some of those big flies had pretty big consequences.

Now, about that catch in the 1954 World Series …

remote and statistical— always threatens its interest, which can be maintained not by the occasional heroics that sportswriters feed upon but by players who always care; who care, that is to say, about themselves and their art."

Hank Aaron understood how to put that caring into practice better than anyone who has ever played the game of baseball. And that makes him a damn worthy all-time home run champion.

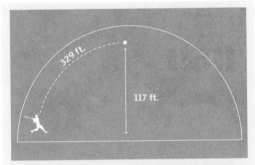

329 ft.

117 ft.

GOING, GOING... NOT GONE!

ON JUNE 10, 1974, Mike Schmidt smashed what some Houston fans consider the hardest ball ever hit in the Astrodome—and it clanged into a speaker hanging from the dome's ceiling. After Schmidt connected off Claude Osteen, the ball he hit smacked the speaker, which was 329 feet from home plate and 117 feet high. But then it dropped into the outfield, Cesar Cedeno retrieved it, and Schmidt was held to a single.

Plays like this were unusually common during the 1960s and early 1970s, when unconventional ground rules at new ballparks and artificial turf (plus indoor obstructions at the Astrodome) combined to produce wacky plays. Of the 24 "lost home runs" described by Bob McConnell and David Vincent in *The Home Run Encyclopedia*—homers credited as other events because of human error—11 were hit between 1963 and 1976.

MOST HOME RUNS BY TWO TEAMMATES, CAREER

No. 1
BRAVES
HANK AARON
EDDIE MATHEWS
859

No. 2
YANKEES
BABE RUTH
LOU GEHRIG
863

No. 3
GIANTS
WILLIE MAYS
WILLIE McCOVEY
814

No. 4
DODGERS/METS
DUKE SNIDER
GIL HODGES
745

No. 5
RED SOX
JIM RICE
DWIGHT EVANS
737

No. 6
SENATORS/TWINS
HARMON KILLEBREW
BOB ALLISON
732

No. 7
CUBS
BILLY WILLIAMS
RON SANTO
713

No. 8
YANKEES
MICKEY MANTLE
YOGI BERRA
702

No. 9
ASTROS
JEFF BAGWELL
CRAIG BIGGIO
689

No. 10
MARINERS
KEN GRIFFEY JR.
JAY BUHNER
667

THE DUO to watch among active players? Atlanta's Joneses, Chipper and Andruw, who had 609 homers as teammates going into 2006. They already hold the record for most dingers by two teammates with the same last name.

Nicknamed The Toy Cannon, Jimmy Wynn stood just 5'9" and weighed, at most, 170 pounds. But like Pedro Martinez today, he was able to generate incredible power from light physique.

ON APRIL 12, 1970, Wynn launched a homer into the leftfield upper deck of the Astrodome—the first batter to do so—prompting the Astros to mark the spot where the ball hit with a cannon stitched into an upholstered seat. "Everybody remembers that more than anything else," said Wynn in 1999, at the last game played at the 'Dome.

Wynn hit .250 for his career, with 291 HR and 964 RBI. Hitters with numbers most similar to those raw totals were generally good but rarely great: Tom Brunansky, Rick Monday, Larry Parrish. But Wynn had a far greater impact than any of his fellow sluggers. The heart of his career was the late 1960s, when runs were harder to come by than Marine enlistees at Ivy League campuses. He spent most of his career in the Astrodome, a phenomenally difficult place to hit for power. In 1967, Wynn went deep 37 times for a Houston team that totaled only 93 homers; in 1968, he hit 26 of the Astros' 66 dingers. He also had played a terrific center field and had outstanding speed.

Snatched away from his hometown Reds by the Houston Colt .45s in the 1962 expansion draft, Wynn had the game-winning hit, a 12th-inning single to score Rusty Staub, in the last regular-season game the team played at Colt Stadium before the team took a new name and moved to the Astrodome in 1965. With 22 HR and 43 SB in 1965, Wynn was the early breakout star on a frontier-town expansion team that also included Staub and Joe Morgan. In 1967, he mashed a series of prodigious taters and raced Hank Aaron for the NL home run title until the final days of the season. One blast on June 10 of that year cleared the left-center scoreboard in Cincinnati entirely and bounced into traffic, leading Astros announcer Loel Passe to exclaim, "That has got to be the longest ball I have ever seen hit in Crosley Field, or hit out of it."

Wynn was both popular and quotable. He once described Sandy Koufax's curveball as a "mystic waterfall." When Houston opened 1969 by going 4–20 in manager Harry "The Hat" Walker's first full season, then went on a hot streak, Wynn said, "We started playing better so Harry would shut up." During

JIMMY WYNN STATS

Year	Team	G	R	HR	RBI	BB	AVG	OPS
1963	Astros	70	31	4	27	30	.244	.691
1964	Astros	67	19	5	18	24	.224	.625
1965	Astros	157	90	22	73	84	.275	.841
1966	Astros	105	62	18	62	41	.256	.761
1967	Astros	158	102	37	107	74	.249	.826
1968	Astros	156	85	26	67	90	.269	.850
1969	Astros	149	113	33	87	148	.269	.943
1970	Astros	157	82	27	88	106	.282	.886
1971	Astros	123	38	7	45	56	.203	.596
1972	Astros	145	117	24	90	103	.273	.860
1973	Astros	139	90	20	55	91	.220	.742
1974	Dodgers	150	104	32	108	108	.271	.884
1975	Dodgers	130	80	18	58	110	.248	.821
1976	Braves	148	75	17	66	127	.207	.744
1977	Yankees/Brewers	66	17	1	13	32	.175	.527
	Career Totals	1920	1105	291	964	1224	.250	.802

off-seasons, Wynn worked as a radio sports broadcaster and a Schlitz beer distributor.

Just before Christmas, 1970, Wynn's wife stabbed him in the stomach during a quarrel the day after their anniversary. Wynn was brandishing a shotgun at the time; his wife didn't know it wasn't loaded. Not seriously injured, Wynn was supposedly recovered by Opening Day, but hit just .203 in 1971. By that time, the Astros were changing from a team with loads of potential into a team that routinely traded away young talent without ever getting over the hump. After Wynn had another off year in 1973, Houston shipped him to the Dodgers for Claude Osteen, who had 180 wins behind him but only 16 left in the tank.

Wynn sparked the 1974 Dodgers to 102 wins and their first pennant since the days of Koufax and Don Drysdale. His teammate Steve Garvey won the MVP, while Wynn earned Comeback Player of the Year honors. But by 1977, his accumulated injuries finally wore him down, and he was finished at age 35.

Oddly, no one has ever paid much attention to Wynn as a Hall of Fame candidate—"oddly," because Wynn's combination of power and walks ought to have earned him more of a cult following by now. Surely Wynn is worth a few of the endless keystrokes pounded on behalf of (or against) Dick Allen.

My opinion is that among centerfielders, five are distinctly better than the rest: Cobb, DiMaggio, Mantle, Mays, and Speaker (in alphabetical order, so as not to start a distracting debate). Duke Snider is not as good as the top five but is better than everyone else. Wynn belongs in the next group of 9 or 10 players.

After his retirement, severe back pain eventually required surgery, and Wynn received help from the Baseball Assistance Team, a group that provides financial support to former big leaguers in need. Happily, he recovered and went on to work as a hitting coach.

Currently, the Toy Cannon is secretary/treasurer for the Major League Baseball Players Alumni Association.

JIMMY WYNN

CHAPTER 5

1977-1992

Balance

On April 6, 1977, Joe Rudi

of the Angels went deep in a 7-0 win against the Mariners' Diego Segui. And as it flew into the Seattle seats, Rudi's Opening Day home run carried the message that baseball was entering a new era.

MIKE SCHMIDT

No. 1
MIKE SCHMIDT
313

No. 2
DALE MURPHY
308

No. 3
EDDIE MURRAY
274

No. 4
DWIGHT EVANS
256

No. 5
ANDRE DAWSON
250

No. 6
DARRELL EVANS
230

No. 7
TONY ARMAS
225

No. 8
LANCE PARRISH
225

No. 9
DAVE WINFIELD
223

No. 10
JACK CLARK
216

MOST HOME RUNS

1980   1989

The dinger was coming back.

To begin with, the Mariners, along with the Toronto Blue Jays, were expansion clubs, and every expansion has been followed by a rise in homers. It's not exactly clear why, but at any given moment, there are probably more minor leaguers (or recent retirees or Caribbean leaguers) who can hit for at least some power than there are pitchers who can get big-league hitters out. So when the number of major-league players increases suddenly, the balance between hitting and pitching tilts toward the guys with the bats.

But while the expansions of the early 1960s added home

MOST TATERS AFTER TURNING 40

1.	Carlton Fisk	72
2.	Darrell Evans	60
3.	Dave Winfield	59
4.	Carl Yastrzemski	49
5.	Stan Musial	46
6.	Ted Williams	44
7.	Hank Aaron	42
8.	Graig Nettles	40
9.	Hank Sauer	39
10T.	Harold Baines	36
10T.	Edgar Martinez	36

LATE AND LONG

BY INNING, by time elapsed, by the farthest stretch of your imagination, the latest home run was conked by Harold Baines on May 9, 1984, to end—finally—a game that began 24 innings and nearly as many hours earlier.

On May 8, the White Sox and the Brewers went into extra innings in Chicago with the score tied 3-3. At 1 a.m., the American League's curfew, the game was suspended until the following afternoon. After play resumed, Milwaukee's Ben Oglivie hit a three-run homer in the top of the 21st, but the Sox managed to score three runs in the bottom of the inning, so the game went on. Finally, with one out in the bottom of the 25th, after eight hours and six minutes of play, Baines, who had been one for nine, took Chuck Porter deep and the White Sox won, 7-6.

(Tom Seaver, who came in to pitch the 25th, picked up the win, then started Chicago's regularly scheduled game that night and notched his second win of the day.)

Baines' homer came on the 753rd pitch of the game.

	INNINGS										R	H	E
MIL	000	000	102	000	000	000	003	000	0	6	20	3
CHI	000	001	002	000	000	000	003	000	1	7	23	1

runs to a game where blasts were already plentiful (and increasing teams in the 1990s would do so again), adding two clubs in 1977 had the effect of helping to bring power back to historically normal levels.

In 1976, the number of major-league homers had fallen to 2,235, the lowest total since 1968. The following season, the rate of home runs per game soared 53 percent in the AL and 47 percent in the NL, with batters crushing a then-record 3,644 dingers. (That mark has since been eclipsed many times.) But all this essentially did was return the home run to the prominence it had enjoyed around, say, 1950 or 1970.

There may have been reasons beyond expansion for the resurgence in home runs.

FACIAL HAIR

APOLOGIES TO DICK ALLEN, a true icono-clast whom *Sports Illustrated* photographed wearing a mustache in the spring of 1970 (but who quickly shaved it off), and to Mark McGwire, whose red beard added to his Paul Bunyan image, but the home run hitter who towers above all others when it comes to facial hair was Reggie Jackson. In 1972, Reggie turned up at spring training sporting a mustache, then surprised the A's by letting it grow until it eventually touched off a revolution in baseball hirsuteness.

Ridiculous though it seems today, at the time Jackson grew his mustache most clubs had policies, formal or informal, against facial hair. (The Yankees, of course, still do.) In fact, no player had worn a mustache during the regular season since Philadelphia A's catcher Wally Schang in 1914. (And his was covered half the time by his mask.)

$300 to any member of the A's who grew a mustache

Neither Oakland owner Charlie Finley nor manager Dick Williams initially liked what they saw on Reggie's lip. But rather than risk Jackson's wrath by demanding a clean shave, the fickle Finley tried a bit of reverse psychology, encouraging Catfish Hunter and other A's pitchers to grow mustaches in an attempt to make Jackson stand out less.

Then Finley decided he actually liked how his players looked, and offered $300 to any member of the A's who grew a mustache by Father's Day, when he planned to hold a Mustache Day promotion. By Father's Day, all 25 A's had mustaches, most notably Rollie Fingers, whose signature handlebar became famous.

So by growing his own mustache, Jackson unintentionally inspired the A's, the most radically individualistic great team of all time, to go hairy together.

In 1977, Rawlings replaced Spalding as the supplier of major league baseballs. Rawlings didn't report any changes in how it was making balls, but it's possible juice was added, purposely or not, somewhere in the manufacturing process. Several teams also took steps to improve visibility for batters at their ballparks. Maybe clubs had grown tired of watching hitters lead the league with 32 homers, which happened three times in the preceding four seasons (1973–1976). If so, the changes, such as blacking out centerfield bleacher seats, had the desired effect: No home run champion has had so few dingers since.

The Mariners played in the Kingdome, a then-new (and now demolished) indoor stadium that was one of the last of the cookie-cutter, multi-purpose facilities built in the 1960s and 1970s. As teams stopped moving to the Sun Belt and the suburbs and started taking root in their new homes, a new, wonderfully diverse kind of baseball emerged. By 1977, some parks were new but others were old; some helped hitters while others favored pitchers; some kept grass while others had artificial turf. With many types of home cooking, all kinds of tastes developed—power flourished, but didn't dominate the game to the exclusion of other talents. In 1977, for example, George Foster hit 52 home runs, but Rod Carew batted .388, Hal McRae hit 54 doubles, Frank Taveras stole 70 bases, and Nolan Ryan struck out 341 hitters. And through the rest of the 1970s and 1980s, mashers and speedsters and high-average hitters and power pitchers co-existed in the game.

In the case of a few particularly great athletes, power and other skills co-existed in the same person. In 1979, George Brett hit 42 doubles, 20 triples, and 23 homers, becoming just the sixth 20-20-20 man in big-league history. The next year,

MAYBE HE SCORED, BUT IT WASN'T A DINGER

ASK 100 PEOPLE to name a song about a home run and probaly 90 will say "Paradise by the Dashboard Light." Meat Loaf's sweaty 1977 opus features an extended baseball-as-sex metaphor, voiced by Phil Rizzuto, and everyone remembers the Scooter exclaiming, "There's the play at the plate ... Holy cow! I think he's gonna make it!" But while the runner (like the singer) is trying to go "all the way," it's not on a home run. He singles to center and takes second when the outfielder bobbles the ball. Then he steals third base, then dashes for home on a squeeze bunt. As Rizzuto's manager, Casey Stengel, used to say, you could look it up.

Rickey Henderson stole 100 bases for the first time, on his way to becoming (temporarily) the greatest power-speed combination of all time. Bo Jackson, who had massive power and terrific speed (but nothing else), made his debut in 1986. In 1988, Jose Canseco posted the first 40-home run/40-stolen base season.

It's true that as the game grew more specialized, a few players emerged who hit home runs and did almost nothing else: Gorman Thomas, Steve Balboni, and Rob Deer, all big swingers, each had seasons playing more than 100 games while batting under .200. But on the whole, this was the age of the multidimensional slugger.

Something else about that forgotten 1977 Angels-Mariners contest: Joe Rudi, California's leftfielder, was also its prize acquisition, signed during the first frenzied winter of real free-agent bidding. Following the 1976 season, 10 months after the Messersmith free-agency ruling in December 1975, clubs really started throwing money at players. Many fans assume that free agency is the reason players move from team to team a lot more often, but there's little evidence of this as a direct effect. Think about it from a franchise's point of view: If you needed a new second baseman before free agency, you traded for one. If you need one now, you can sign one. But there's no reason, necessarily, that you're going to be looking for new players more frequently. Dave Kingman didn't homer for four different teams in 1977 because of free agency, but because three teams in quick succession wanted to get rid of him.

Free agency's real impact has actually been on the lengths of players' careers: Now that players are raking in a much bigger share of baseball's revenues than they were 30 years ago, they have much more incentive to keep themselves healthy and

CONTINUED ON PAGE 131

in *How Life Imitates the World Series*
by Thomas Boswell
This chapter is about the 1978 Yankees-Red Sox divisional
playoff game—and the most
infamous dinger in Fenway Park history.

- -

WHEN [BUCKY] DENT dragged his bat to home plate with two out and two men on base in the Yankee seventh, then fouled the second pitch off his foot, hopping out of the batter's box in pain, he looked as ineffectual and inconspicuous as a CIA agent with a bomb in his briefcase. Normally, the worrywart [Carlton] Fisk uses such delays to visit his pitcher …

But for Dent, what's the worry?

As Dent was administered a pain-killing spray, on-deck hitter [Mickey] Rivers, who had forgotten his sunglasses and butchered a flyball earlier, became uncharacteristically observant. He saw a crack in Dent's bat and fetched him another one of the same style. Of such minutiae is history made. That and fastballs down the middle.

"After Dent hit it," said Fisk," I let out a sigh of relief. I thought, 'We got away with that mistake pitch.' I almost screamed at Mike [Torrez]."

"Then I saw Yaz looking up and I said, 'Oh, God.'"

Several innings before, the wind had reversed and was blowing toward the left-field corner. [Carl] Yastrzemski watched that boosting wind loft the ball barely over the wall, fair by 30 feet. As the three-run homer nestled in the net, Yastrzemski's knees buckled as though he had been hammered over the head with a bat.

The Yankees erupted from the dugout like souls released from Hades. What followed seemed as inexorable as a shark eating the leg after it tastes the foot.

HR CHAMPS
BA CHUMPS

.242
HARMON KILLEBREW (42)
Senators, 1959

.204

DAVE KINGMAN (37HR)
METS, 1982

.232
GAVVY CRAVATH (8)
Phillies, 1918

.241
FRED ODWELL (9)
Reds, 1905

MOST OF THE PLAYERS on this list of league HR leaders who carded the 10 worst batting averages in history were simply power hitters having off years. A few had at least some compensating defensive value, if only the ability to play a position without falling down too often. But none came close to Dave Kingman in being so utterly inept in all facets of the game save one: hitting the ball out of the park. Want proof?

Sky King was batting .199 on September 1, 1982. He had just nine doubles and one triple in 535 at bats that year; no other home run champion has ever had so few non-HR extra-base hits. He struck out a career-high 156 times. He committed 18 errors and—because of his amazingly

ungraceful way of bending on one knee to take infielders' throws and then bungling them—helped other Mets infielders lead the majors in combined errors.

None of the other HR champs/BA chumps ever stunk up the joint (except in the Dinger Department) the way Kingman did in 1982. That same year, AL HR leader Gorman Thomas hit only .245 but socked two more homers, had 30 other extra-base hits, and drew 25 more walks.

The best comparison might be with a guy named Tim Jordan, who was a tall first baseman for Brooklyn when the team was called the Superbas nearly a century ago. Jordan was one of the few players in the Deadball Era with enough clout to clear the fences. (Ty Cobb led the AL with nine homers in 1909, all of them inside-the-parkers. Of course,

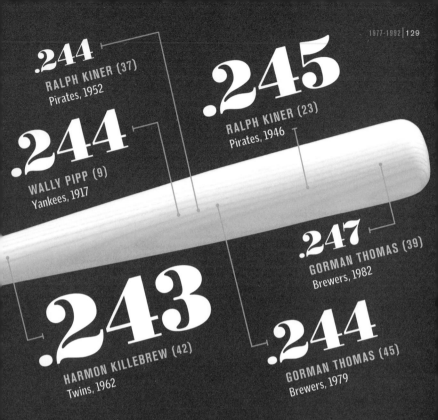

.244
RALPH KINER (37)
Pirates, 1952

.245
RALPH KINER (23)
Pirates, 1946

.244
WALLY PIPP (9)
Yankees, 1917

.247
GORMAN THOMAS (39)
Brewers, 1982

.243
HARMON KILLEBREW (42)
Twins, 1962

.244
GORMAN THOMAS (45)
Brewers, 1979

he also hit .377.) Jordan led the NL with 12 homers in 1908, depriving Honus Wagner, who hit 10 HR and led the league in just about everything else, of the Triple Crown. But Jordan hit .247 that year.

Kingman was famous—or infamous—for a lot of things: a monster 48-HR (.288!) season with the Cubs in 1979; a 530-foot Wrigley Field bomb in 1976 that hit the third house beyond Waveland Avenue; a monumental surliness towards management, fans, and (especially) media; dumping a bucket of ice water on a reporter to demonstrate his displeasure with something the reporter wrote; and having a live rat in a gift box delivered to a female reporter who offended him when he was with the A's in 1986 by daring to enter the Oakland clubhouse.

Nor was Kong exactly beloved by his teammates. "He has the personality of a tree trunk," said Mets catcher John Stearns. Kingman evoked another image from Cubs reliever Bill Caudill: "He was like a cavity that made your whole mouth sore."

After swatting 35 homers (with a .210 BA) in 1986, Kingman did not receive a contract offer for the following season. This was the era of collusion, so maybe all the teams in the majors conspired against him. (The arbitration board established to review cases of alleged collusion thought so: Kingman was later awarded $829,850 in damages.)

Or maybe not. Maybe every team in baseball took a long, independent look at what the most one-dimensional power hitter in history brought to the party and simply decided, each on its own ... uh, no.

The Crowd Was Ready...

from *REGGIE: THE AUTOBIOGRAPY*

by Reggie Jackson with Mike Lupica

SETTING: JUST BEFORE GAME SIX of the 1977 World Series, the Yankees are up 3-2 over the Dodgers. Reggie Jackson, who had homered on his last swing in Game 5—a 10-4 Dodgers laugher—reflects on how he felt before going out that crisp October night to make history.

I should have known in batting practice. But batting practice can be tricky sometimes. You can hit ball after ball into the seats, feel like you're on top of the world, want the game to start right now. The next thing you're doing is sitting in front of your locker after the game, munching on a piece of chicken, and wondering where the oh-for-four came from. ...

Batting practice can confuse the hell out of you.

But BP on October 18 was something special. I cannot ever remember having one like it. The players around the batting cage were amazed, and so were the writers. The crowd, especially out in right field, was going crazy ... I hit maybe 40 balls during my time in the cage. I must have hit 20

into the seats. Upper deck. Bullpen. Into the black in center. Didn't matter. The baseball looked like a volleyball to me.

Willie Randolph came up to me finally and said, "Would you do us all a favor and maybe save a little of that?"

I laughed. I knew I felt gooooood.

"There's more where that came from," I said. ... I've had great batting practices in the past; I got a standing ovation one time in Detroit when I finished. This was different. By the time I was done, it wasn't just the people out in right. Everyone in the ballpark was whooping and hollering. We were ready. The crowd was ready.

And so was I.

OUTCOME: On three pitches, from three pitchers, Jackson hit three home runs, as the Yankees won the 1977 World Series. The following the day, the entire front page of New York's *Daily News* was taken up by a photo of Jackson in right field in the ninth inning, his back to the camera, waving to the crowd. Superimposed on it was a three-word banner headline: REG-gie! REG-gie! REG-gie!

Jackson summed up his performance this way: "Don Larsen had his perfect game in 1956. I had mine in 1977. Three swings. Three dingers."

REGGIE. REGGIE. REGGIE.

. in shape to squeeze every last game they can out of their talent. And in the late 1970s and 1980s, players began setting all kinds of home run records related to longevity. Eddie Murray, who came up in 1977, played for 21 years and cracked 504 home runs without ever hitting 35 in a single season. Dave Winfield went deep 465 times between 1973 and 1995 without ever leading the league. Ken Griffey Sr. wasn't a power hitter, but he hung around long enough that at the age of 40, on September 14, 1990,

he and Ken Griffey Jr. became the first father and son ever to hit back-to-back homers.

This era, when homers were enjoyably frequent, produced some of the most memorable fluke home runs of all time.

Bucky Dent, the last Yankee anyone expected to go yard, shattered the hopes of Red Sox fans in the 1978 playoff for the AL East title.

In 1983, George Brett drove a Rich Gossage fastball deep into the rightfield seats at Yankee Stadium, apparently giving Kansas

CONTINUED ON PAGE 134

MOST TIMES LEADING LEAGUE IN HOME RUNS

12 BABE RUTH

8 MIKE SCHMIDT

7 RALPH KINER

6 GAVVY CRAVATH

6 HARMON KILLEBREW

6 MEL OTT

5 HARRY STOVEY

4 16 PLAYERS, MOST RECENTLY ALEX RODRIGUEZ

No. 1 **13**	No. 2 **12**	No. 3T **11**	No. 3T **11**
Alfonso Soriano **2003** YANKEES	Brady Anderson **1996** ORIOLES	Bobby Bonds **1973** GIANTS	Jacque Jones **2002** TWINS

MOST LEADOFF HOME RUNS, *Season*

RICKEY HENDERSON will be best remembered for his stolen bases, style, and runs scored—probably in that order (though they shouldn't be). But Henderson's power was something special, too. Simply put, he was a better slugger than anyone who remained a leadoff hitter throughout his career. In 1986, Henderson hit 28 home runs while stealing 87 bases, combining those two stats better than anyone ever had. (See chapter 6 for an ex-planation of Power/Speed Number, and to find out who eclipsed Henderson's blended total.) And with 297 career homers to go with his record 1,406 stolen bases, he ranked as the best dual threat in the game between the time of Willie Mays and the era of Barry Bonds.

On October 4, 2001, in the third inning of a game against the Dodgers, Henderson homered off the top of the leftfield fence in San Diego. The run scored gave him 2,246 for his career, breaking Ty Cobb's all-time record—

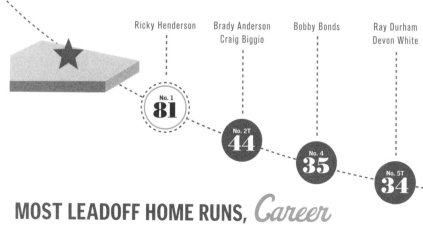

	Ricky Henderson	Brady Anderson Craig Biggio	Bobby Bonds	Ray Durham Devon White
	No. 1 **81**	No. 2T **44**	No. 4 **35**	No. 5T **34**

MOST LEADOFF HOME RUNS, *Career*

No. 5T
9

No. 5T
9

No. 5T
9

Brad Wilkerson
2004
EXPOS

Rickey Henderson
1986
YANKEES

Ray Durham
2004
GIANTS

and he scored it by sliding into home plate.

The Associated Press reported what happened next:

"Since Henderson couldn't rip out home plate and hold it over his head, which he did with third base when he became all-time steals leader in 1991, [Tony] Gwynn presented him a gilded major league home plate with a plaque marking the milestone. So Henderson held that over his head instead. Henderson then answered a curtain call, bowing to the fans and blowing kisses."

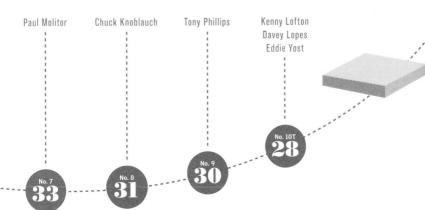

Paul Molitor

Chuck Knoblauch

Tony Phillips

Kenny Lofton
Davey Lopes
Eddie Yost

No. 10T
28

No. 7
33

No. 8
31

No. 9
30

City a 5-4 lead over New York—only to have the Yankees challenge the dinger because of how much pine tar Brett had on his bat. Home plate umpire Tim McClelland called Brett out, whereupon Brett charged out of the dugout looking completely insane. The Royals held him back, protested the ruling, got the dinger reinstated, and won the game when the teams finished it 25 days later.

Around 3 a.m. on July 5, 1985, Rick Camp, a Braves pitcher with a .074 lifetime batting average, cracked a solo in the 18th inning of a game against the Mets. (The smash tied the score at 11-11, but Camp lost the game in the following inning.)

In 1987, home runs skyrocketed, leading to much discussion about whether balls were juiced. But the phenomenon turned out to be just a one-season fluke when dingers dropped back in 1988. On the whole in those days, home runs were to baseball as walnuts are to a perfectly-baked chocolate chip cookie: They

THREE GRAND SLAMS IN A GAME

THREE PLAYERS hit grand slams in one game for the first time on August 6, 1986, when Bobby Valentine's Rangers visited Earl Weaver's Orioles. In the second inning, Texas' Toby Harrah cleared the bases with a blast off Ken Dixon (who would also be the starter the following year when Toronto hit 10 homers in a game).

Baltimore roared back in the fourth, when Larry Sheets connected for a slam against Bobby Witt to plate four of the Orioles' nine runs in the inning. After Witt surrendered another hit, Jeff Russell came in and gave up two walks sandwiched around two outs. Then Cal Ripken reached on an error, setting the stage for Jim Dwyer to crack the game's third grand slam.

Baltimore could have used another slam, as Texas rallied to win 13-11.

Less than a year later, it happened again in a classic Wrigley Field game on June 3, 1987. Cubs outfielder Brian Dayett hit a one-out slam off Houston lefty Bob Knepper in the first inning, part of an assault that saw the Cubs score nine runs against the Astros starter that inning. Houston's Billy Hatcher returned the favor in the fourth, going yard with the bases loaded against Rick Sutcliffe. And in the sixth, Ryne Sandberg singled to right, Jody Davis doubled to left, Dayett walked, and Keith Moreland drilled his second homer and the third grand slam of the game.

Final score: Cubs 22, Astros 7. (Yes, the wind was blowing out.)

INNINGS	**1**			**3**						R	H	E
T E X	0	5	1	0	0	0	0	6	1	13	19	1
B A L	0	0	0	9	0	2	0	0	0	11	7	0

2

INNINGS		**2**								R	H	E
H O U	2	0	0	4	1	0	0	0	0	7	9	2
C H I	9	2	2	1	2	4	2	0	X	22	21	0

1   **3**

GREATEST HOME RUN

CALLS

A GREAT CALL of a historic home run should combine the reactions of both reporter and fans—it should explain the trajectory of the hit and the significance of the event at hand, but also convey how astonishing and thrilling the homer was. A baseball version of, "One small step for man, one giant leap for mankind," only with more passion.

"The Giants win the pennant! The Giants win the pennant!" by Russ Hodges after Bobby Thomson beat the Dodgers in 1951 is the most famous call ever, but let's face it, he just screamed the same phrase over and over again into his radio microphone.

When Roger Maris broke Babe Ruth's single-season record in 1961, Phil Rizzuto yelled, "Holy Cow, he did it! Sixty-one home runs! They're fighting for the ball out there!"

And when Hank Aaron passed Ruth's lifetime total in 1974, Braves radio announcer Milo Hamilton exclaimed, "It's gone! It's 715! There's a new home run champion of all time, and it's Henry Aaron!"

It's nice that these announcers were rooting for their teams' players, but those were pretty generic calls. No baseball announcer had ever been as poetic yet acute as Al Michaels asking and answering, "Do you believe in miracles? Yes!" when the 1980 U.S. Olympic hockey team beat the Soviet Union.

And then Jack Buck did it three times in half a dozen years.

1985: The NL Championship Series between the Dodgers and Cardinals was tied, two games apiece, and Game 5 was also knotted, 2-2, when Ozzie Smith came to bat in the bottom of the ninth. Buck's call on KMOX radio in St. Louis went like this:

"Smith corks one into right down the line! It may go! Go crazy, folks, go crazy! It's a home run and the Cardinals have won the game by the score of 3-2 on a home run by the Wizard!"

1988: The Dodgers were trailing the heavily favored Athletics in the first game of the World Series, 4-3, in the bottom of the ninth. With two outs and a runner on, A's relief ace (and control artist) Dennis Eckersley walked Mike Davis, who hit .196 that season. Then Kirk Gibson, who hadn't started the game because of hamstring and knee injuries, stepped to the plate. Buck's call on CBS Radio went like this:

"Gibson swings! And a fly ball to deep right field! This is gonna be a home run! Unbelievable! A home run for Gibson! And the Dodgers have won the game, 5-4! I don't believe what I just saw!"

1991: The sixth game of the World Series went into extra innings, with the Twins needing a win to stave off elimination by the Braves. Kirby Puckett led off the bottom of the 11th against Charlie Leibrandt. Buck's call on CBS Television went like this:

"And we'll see you tomorrow night!"

The gravelly-voiced, briskly-paced Buck was a St. Louis institution for nearly five decades until his death in 2002. But he was also something of an "emcee for the guy dressed in a dinner jacket," as Skip Caray once called him.

When Buck let his surprise show and his emotions fly, he made calls worthy of three of the most dramatic home runs in history.

10

BIG FLIES, ONLY ONE GAME

KNOW HOW AGGRESSIVE a flock of Blue Jays get when they get riled? Consider this: On September 14, 1987, six Toronto hitters went deep against the Orioles: Ernie Whitt (three times), Rance Mulliniks (twice), Lloyd Moseby, George Bell (twice), and Rob Ducey and Fred McGriff (once each). A record 10 round-trippers off five Orioles pitchers, including three off starter and loser Ken Dixon. The Jays won, 18-3, but they should have saved some of that long ball mojo. After going up by 2 1/2 games in the AL East with a week to play, the Jays lost their last seven and finished second to Detroit.

provided pleasant, indeed essential, flavor without calling undue attention to themselves.

Mike Schmidt was the dominant slugger of the time, to an extent that might surprise even serious fans. Schmidt led his league in homers eight times, more than anyone besides Babe Ruth—a pretty astonishing stat. Because he hit .196 in 1973 and struck out 180 times in 1975 and because they eat their young, Philadelphia fans chose not to notice that Schmidt in his 20s put together a string of seasons that were among the best by any third baseman in history.

Instead, they were busy booing him for his horrendous post-season performances from 1976 to 1978, when the Phillies won three NL East titles but never made it to the World Series. But with 45 homers in 1979, back-to-back MVPs in 1980 and 1981, 40 more dingers in 1983, and another MVP in 1986, Schmidt

CONTINUED ON PAGE 140

MOST GRAND SLAMS, SEASON

DON MATTINGLY launched a record-setting campaign on May 14, 1987, by clearing the bases for the first time in his career. He slammed again on June 29, and then twice more in July during his record-tying streak of homering in eight consecutive games.

Then on September 25, with the sacks full of Yankees in the second inning, Hit Man went deep again against Baltimore's Jose Mesa, who started five games as a rookie and who enjoyed serving up taters back then as much as he would coming out of the bullpen in later years.

With that fifth grand salami, Mattingly tied the mark set by Ernie Banks (1955) and Jim Gentile (1961). He broke the record four days later, slamming Bruce Hurst of the Red Sox.

Mattingly never hit another grand slam.

Everyone has his or her own favorite statistic,

whether it's traditional or invented; it's hard-wired into the DNA of every baseball fan. (My own is runs scored divided by hits—make a best-of list some time and see what you find.) But there's one measure that grew very popular in the 1970s and 1980s and is still floating around the ether that is so dumb that nobody should still be using it. That stat is Runs Produced.

In the days before sabermetrics developed a mass audience, when fans and sportswriters needed an easy way to sum up players' numbers for purposes of comparison, it became common to add together a batter's runs and RBI. And then someone—Bill James once blamed Spiro Agnew—decided to subtract home runs,

On June 27, 1970, in the fifth inning of a game against Houston, Reds pitcher Jim Merritt struck out and Pete Rose hit a grounder to first. Bobby Tolan walked, stole second and scored on a Tony Perez single. Then Johnny Bench grounded out to end the inning.

So the Reds scored one run but had two runs produced—one run scored (Tolan) + one RBI (Perez) - no home runs.

The following day, Rose and Tolan led off the final game of the series with back-to-back homers. (That was the third time they had done that, the most ever by any duo, but that's not my point.) Cincinnati didn't score again that inning.

So this time, the Reds scored two runs

THE STUPID STAT THAT DISSES DINGERS

because, the "thinking" went, you wouldn't want to count the same run twice.

So in 1988, when Darryl Strawberry scored 101 runs, hit 39 homers, and drove in 101, he had 163 runs produced—101 + 101 - 39 = 163. Kirk Gibson had 106 runs scored, 25 HR, and 76 RBI, for 157 runs produced. People would take those numbers as a starting point in MVP discussions, then talk about how to account for defense and leadership.

Except the part about not counting the same runs twice doesn't make any sense. Runs and RBI already count each run twice—once when it's scored, and once when it's driven in. Subtracting home runs just penalizes, for no good reason, the players who hit them.

Here's an example from the real world.

and had two runs produced—two runs scored (Rose, Tolan) + two RBI (Rose, Tolan) - the two home runs.

Huh? The Reds scored twice as many runs in the second case as in the first, and any stat worthy of the name should reflect that reality. But Rose and Tolan each lost a run produced in the second example because they committed the act of driving themselves in. Isn't that a good thing, not a bad thing?

So now you know. If you hear anyone talking about "runs produced" on sports radio, pull over to the side of the road, call in, and explain why the so-called statistic is biased against power hitters. Anybody using runs and RBI to make arguments should just add the two together and leave well enough alone.

MOST HOME RUNS
CAREER
MINOR LEAGUES

484
HECTOR ESPINO
1960-1984

432
BUZZ ARLETT
1918-1937

420
NICK CULLOP
1920-1944

400
MERV CONNORS
1934-1953

THE MEXICAN LEAGUE and Major League Baseball went to war in the 1940s, when Commissioner Happy Chandler suspended big-leaguers like Sal Maglie and Mickey Owen for jumping their contracts to head south of the border. But in 1955, the Mexican League joined the National Association, and other Mexican circuits soon followed, so player statistics from the Mexican League are included in organized baseball's minor league totals.

As a consequence, this list is dominated by two types of players: Americans from the 1920s and 1930s, when one-dimensional power hitters could have long minor-league careers; and Mexican sluggers, who often start young and play forever. (All 10 players on the list, by the way, hit significantly more homers than the 247 that Crash Davis, supposedly the all-time minor league king, said he had in Bull Durham.)

HECTOR ESPINO, known as the Mexican Babe Ruth, at one time held the Mexican League single-season record for home runs and career records for games played, runs, hits, doubles, home runs, total bases, and RBI. Those have all since been broken, but he's still the all-time home run champion of the minor leagues. Espino was the Mexican League Rookie of the Year in 1962, and in 1964, he hit .371 with 46 homers—at the time, a Mexican League record. That drew the attention of the Cardinals, who signed him late in the season and sent him to AAA Jacksonville, where he hit .300 with three homers in 32 games. St. Louis invited Espino to spring training the following year, but he declined. And he never returned to play in the United States, despite attempts by the Angels to sign him in the late 1960s. Homesickness, racism, a preference for being a big star—different sources (including Espino himself, over the years) offer

different reasons for his failure to pursue the golden ring north of the border.

A 5'11" righty, Espino won four home run titles and five batting championships in Mexico. He played until he was 45 and is in the Caribbean as well as Mexican Halls of Fame. He died of a heart attack in 1997. In Hermosillo, a baseball hotbed where Fernando Valenzuela finished out his pitching days, the ballpark is named after Espino.

JACK PIERCE, who broke Espino's single-season Mexican League HR record, had the benefit of a juiced ball, but was nevertheless a classic minor league slugger. Pierce spent four seasons in the Braves' system before heading to Mexico at age 25 in 1974. He got an extended look with the Tigers the following year, and he cracked eight homers but hit just .235 with 40 strikeouts in 170 at-bats. He played in Puebla in 1976, leading the Mexican League in homers, and

in Nankai, Japan, in 1977. He then returned to Mexico and played long enough to enjoy the lively ball that the Mexican League introduced in 1984. In 1986, at the age of 38, Pierce slammed 54 homers, a Mexican League record that still stands. He retired after the 1987 season with more home runs in Mexico than any American-born player.

In 1984, his 11th season of pro ball, NELSON BARRERA hit .354 with 20 homers, earning him a shot with Buffalo, then a AAA team for the White Sox. But he hit .176 in the United States and returned to Mexico. There he kept blasting home runs for a long time. He led the league with 42 in 1987, and still had enough oomph to crack 23 in 2000 at age 42. In July 2002, Barrera was player-manager of his hometown team in Campeche, and was just five home runs shy of Espino's all-time minor-league mark. But while he was repairing his roof, he touched a high-voltage cable and was killed.

indisputably became the best third baseman of all time (even if Pete Rose unfairly got the lion's share of credit for leading the Phillies to a world championship in 1980).

LEADING OFF
BACK-TO-BACK-TO-BACK
- - - - - - - - - - - - - - - - - - - -

ONLY ONCE HAS A TEAM has led off a game with three straight home runs, and it was a strange trio of hitters not known for power who did it.

On April 13, 1987, in the bottom of the first inning of San Diego's home opener against the Giants, Marvell Wynne cracked a homer off Roger Mason. Then Tony Gwynn went yard. Then John Kruk followed with another shot. The Padres lost anyway, 13-6, and went on to finish last, which is what you get for batting Marvell Wynne leadoff.

Based on their career rates of home runs per plate appearance, the odds that Wynne, Gwynn, and Kruk would go deep consecutively were about 250,000 to 1.

Schmidt, who early in his career was a friend and ally of the iconoclastic Dick Allen and who later clashed with manager Dallas Green and GM Paul "the Pope" Owens, was never a management favorite. And even when the Philadelphia fans came around to respecting him, they found him easy to admire but hard to love. Schmidt was extremely intense and unsentimental: Referring to his own relentless study and practice habits, he has called himself the Nick Faldo of baseball. But by all accounts, Schmidt was a good teammate. And he led the league in slugging five times and on-base percentage three times while winning 10 Gold Gloves. In 2002, Allen Barra wrote that you could make an argument for Schmidt as player of the 20th century—and Barra wasn't laughed out of sportswriting.

The year after Schmidt retired, George Will examined the state of baseball, discussing players as craftsmen, in a tendentious tome called *Men at Work*. At one point he compared the artistry of Tony Gwynn with the power of Harmon Killebrew: "Killebrew, who hit more home runs than anyone else in the 1960s, is a suitable symbol of big bang baseball: 8,147 at bats, zero sacrifices. Gwynn, with his high average and large number of stolen bases, is a suitable symbol of the direction in which baseball has moved."

Like any good conservative, Will was looking backward. As he published those words, the Oakland A's were already revolutionizing strength conditioning in baseball. And the men who supplied their biggest stars with performance enhancers were about to give home run totals a boost, this time to unhealthy levels.

JIM RICE was the most feared hitter in baseball in his day, the kind of slugger who won fans over because they believed he delivered in crucial situations. That says a lot about the time and place in which he played.

Born in Anderson, South Carolina, Rice was picked by the Red Sox in the first round of the 1971 draft. Three years later, he won the International League's Triple Crown, batting .337 with 25 home runs and 93 RBI for Pawtucket. In a 67-AB September stint in the Show, he drove in 13 runs. When Fred Lynn hit .419 during his own cup of coffee that month, Red Sox fans stirred with hope. The two young outfielders didn't disappoint, leading Boston to an American League pennant and World Series appearance against the Big Red Machine in 1975. Although his breakout season (.309 BA with 22 homers and 102 RBI) was only slightly overshadowed by Lynn's (.331 with 47 doubles, 21 dingers, and 105 RBI), Rice, who finished second to Lynn in the AL Rookie of the Year vote and third behind Lynn and John Mayberry in the MVP balloting, felt slighted by the endless comparisons to his fence-crashing centerfield teammate.

At 6'2" and 205 pounds, Rice had enormous strength. In 1975, he was one of just six batters to smash a ball over the wall to the right of Fenway's centerfield flagpole. (He was also the last; Boston's big scoreboard went up before the next season.) In 1977, he started a three-year streak in which he had at least 39 home runs and more than 200 hits. And in 1978, he did all a guy could do to carry a team to a championship, leading the league in home runs (46) and triples (15) as well as hits and RBI while playing every game

for a Boston team that was damaged by injuries. On his way to the AL MVP, Rice amassed 406 total bases, the most in the major leagues in 30 years. Thirty of his 46 dingers either tied games or put Boston ahead. Ultimately, though, he could not lift the Red Sox past the Yankees in the division-deciding playoff game.

Rice had off years in 1980 (when he was hurt) and 1981 (when there was a strike). By then, there was a permanent divide between him and the Boston media. Rice wasn't actively hostile to sportswriters, but he didn't go out of his way to talk to them. He disliked criticism, and his personality, which seemed to range from private to sullen to glowering, didn't invite intimate exchanges. As important as Rice was to the Red Sox, they were never really "his" team.

Race was one reason for this. Boston was in the midst of a divisive busing crisis when Rice's career began, and remained an intensely polarized city through the late 1970s and early 1980s. And the Red Sox, the last major-league team to integrate, had a long, sorry record on race relations. In Winter Haven, Florida, where the team trained, white players were allowed to eat for free at the local Elks Club while blacks were barred from entering. Rice told a reporter about this in 1979, but the story didn't break in the Boston press until 1985. After the 1985 season, the Sox fired Tommy Harper, the coach who had complained publicly about the practice during spring training.

Rice seemed to view these kinds of things as predestined, an occasion for further resignation and quiet bitterness. "I'm used to Boston," he once said. "What people think of me comes with the job. It bothers me—of course, it bothers me, because it'd bother everyone—but

JIM RICE

JIM RICE STATS

Year	Team	G	R	HR	RBI	BB	AVG	OPS
1974	Red Sox	24	6	1	13	4	.269	.680
1975	Red Sox	144	92	22	102	36	.309	.841
1976	Red Sox	153	75	25	85	28	.282	.797
1977	Red Sox	160	104	39	114	53	.320	.969
1978	Red Sox	163	121	46	139	58	.315	.970
1979	Red Sox	158	117	39	130	57	.325	.977
1980	Red Sox	124	81	24	86	30	.294	.840
1981	Red Sox	108	51	17	62	34	.284	.775
1982	Red Sox	145	86	24	97	55	.309	.868
1983	Red Sox	155	90	39	126	52	.305	.911
1984	Red Sox	159	98	28	122	44	.280	.791
1985	Red Sox	140	85	27	103	51	.291	.836
1986	Red Sox	157	98	20	110	62	.324	.874
1987	Red Sox	108	66	13	62	45	.277	.766
1988	Red Sox	135	57	15	72	48	.264	.736
1989	Red Sox	56	22	3	28	13	.234	.621
	Career Totals	2089	1249	382	1451	670	.298	.854

there's just nothing you can do about it. You can just roll with the punches."

In retrospect, the value of the numbers Rice put up, especially in his 30s, is suspect. In the 1970s and 1980s, newspapers generally ran lists of league leaders once a week, focusing on the Triple Crown categories, and that was how fans (and many baseball executives) got their information. This played to Rice's strengths: home runs, batting average, and RBI. But his totals were helped by Fenway—in 1977 and again in 1979, 27 of his 39 taters came at home. He also grounded into close to 20 double plays a year, and, most important, he made a ton of outs. Rice hit .298 lifetime but had an on-base percentage of .352. From 1982 through 1985, he amassed 448 RBI but was not a great hitter. He did have a last hurrah in 1986, when he started hitting the other way more frequently, posted another 200-hit season, and helped the Red Sox win another pennant. But the Hall of Fame verdict on him—a near-miss—is not unfair.

In 1989, Red Sox manager Joe Morgan sent Spike Owen to pinch-hit for Rice in a bunt situation, and Rice exploded. Injured for most of that season, he hit only three homers and didn't play after August 3. He was insulted when the Red Sox released him: He was told his option for 1990 wasn't going to be picked up a few hours before the September 25 game at Fenway against the Yankees. Boston made matters worse by asking him to share a day in his honor with Bob Stanley. After a few years in exile, Rice came back to the Red Sox as a hitting coach, and is now a pre- and postgame commentator for the New England Sports Network.

MARK McGWIRE

CHAPTER 6

1993-2004

Hyper-inflation

Sometimes a statistic can tell a story better than any anecdote. In all of major league history, from 1876 through 1994, players hit 50 or more home runs in a season 18 times.

1876-1919   1920-1945   1846-1962   1963-1976   1977-1992   **1993-2004**   2005-

In just the eight seasons

since 1994—that is, from 1995 through 2002—it happened 19 times again.

SWITCH SWATS IN SAME STANZA

PLAYERS HAVE HIT home runs from both sides of the plate in the same game on more then 200 occasions. Only twice has a batter done it in one inning. On April 8, 1993, switch-hitter Carlos Baerga of the Indians went deep off lefthander Steve Howe and righthander Steve Farr in the seventh inning of a 15-5 win against the Yankees. And in the fourth inning of a Cubs-Brewers game on August 29, 2002, Chicago's Mark Bellhorn, batting righty, hit a two-run shot off Andrew Lorraine, then turned around and slammed a three-run dinger off Jose Cabrera. The Cubs won, 15-10.

Baseball's contemporary power surge actually ignited in 1993, when the National League expanded to 14 teams and MLB opened shop in the thin air of Denver. Home runs jumped 55 percent in the NL and 17 percent in the AL, to a total of 4,030. And the hits just kept on coming. In the strike-shortened 1994 season, Jeff Bagwell (1.201) and Frank Thomas (1.217) posted gargantuan OPS. Matt Williams, with 43 homers, was on pace to tie Roger Maris' single-season record when games stopped, and Ken Griffey Jr., Bagwell, and Thomas weren't far behind.

Now, it's true that having 81 games a year in Colorado has added a passel of dingers to the game. Coors Field typically increases scoring by a whopping 25 to 30 percent a year, producing all kinds of fun distortions. In 1995, the Rockies became the second team (after the 1977 Dodgers) with four players to hit 30 or more home runs: Dante Bichette, Larry Walker, Vinny Castilla, and Andres Galarraga. The following year, they became the second club (after the 1973 Braves) to feature three 40-homer hitters—Galarraga, Ellis Burks, and Castilla—with Bichette chipping in 31. And the year after that, a different member of the Rockies led the NL in dingers for the third straight season (Walker, following Galarraga and Bichette).

But by 1996, it was becoming clear that the game's power jolt was a bigger deal than any temporary increase associated with expansion, and that it wasn't confined to mile-high conditions. Brady Anderson—Brady Anderson?—smacked 50 home runs, including a then-record 12 leadoff dingers. Three teams bashed more homers than the 1961 Yankees. And the overall

CONTINUED ON PAGE 150

No. 1
MARK McGWIRE
405

No. 2
KEN GRIFFEY JR.
382

No. 3
BARRY BONDS
361

No. 4
ALBERT BELLE
351

No. 5
JUAN GONZALEZ
339

No. 6
SAMMY SOSA
332

No. 7
RAFAEL PALMEIRO
328

No. 8
JOSE CANSECO
303

No. 9
FRANK THOMAS
301

No. 10T
MATT WILLIAMS
300

No. 10T
FRED McGRIFF
300

MOST HOME RUNS

1990 1999

No. 1	No. 2	No. 3	No. 4	No. 5
43.91 Alex Rodriguez 1998 42 HR/46 SB	**42.53** Eric Davis 1987 37 HR/50 SB	**42.36** Rickey Henderson 1986 28 HR/87 SB	**40.98** Barry Bonds 1996 42 HR/40 SB	**40.98** Jose Canseco 1988 42 HR/40 SB

POWER AND SPEED

It's a lot of fun to hook together stats for power and speed. They seem like opposite skills, so the players who demonstrate both in abundance fit our intuitive image of the complete athlete.

Only three players have ever led the league in both home runs and stolen bases. Two were Deadball Era stars: Jimmy Sheckard for the Superbas (think Dodgers) in 1903 (9/67) and Ty Cobb for the Tigers in 1909 (9/76).

The third was Chuck Klein, who belted 38 taters and swiped 20 bags for the Phillies in 1932. Klein put up huge numbers when the entire National League was hitting close to .280. He led the NL with 43 homers in 1929; had 250 hits, including 59 doubles, in 1930; led the league in runs, home runs, and RBI in 1931; won the MVP along with his home run and stolen base crowns in 1932; and won the Triple Crown in 1933. It's true that Klein perfected the art of knocking balls over the right-field wall at the Baker Bowl, which was just 280 feet from home plate at the foul pole, but nobody else in the live ball era has ever managed, in any park, to lead his league in dingers as well as stolen bases in the same year.

Willie Mays came the closest: In 1955, his 51 HR topped the NL, but the Braves' Bill Bruton edged him by one stolen base, 25 to 24.

Mays is also the only batter, other than Cubs outfielder Frank "Wildfire" Schulte, to hit at least 20 homers, 20 doubles, and 20 triples while stealing 20 or more bases in one season. (Mays did it in 1957, Wildfire in 1911.)

Until the 1970s, Mays was the only marquee member of the 30/30 Club. In 1922, the Browns' Ken Williams hit 39 homers and stole 37 bases, becoming the first player to pass 30 in both categories in the same year. Mays did it twice (1956 and 1957), followed by Hank Aaron (1963), Bobby Bonds (1969), and Tommy Harper (1970).

Since the early 1990s, 30/30 seasons have become much more common. Each year from 1996 through 2005 has at least one, including 30/30 campaigns by Dante Bichette and Jose

No. 10	No. 9	No. 8	No. 7	No. 6
319.61 Paul Molitor 234 HR 504 SB	**324.56** Reggie Jackson 563 HR 228 SB	**334.22** Sammy Sosa 588 HR 234 SB	**364.22** Hank Aaron 755 HR 240 SB	**365.78** Andre Dawson 438 HR 314 SB

Cruz Jr.—fine players, but not guys whom anybody ever confused with Willie Mays.

To date, Jose Canseco, Barry Bonds, and Alex Rodriguez are the only members of the exclusive 40/40 Club. (40/40 Club, incidentally, is the name of hip-hop mogul Jay-Z's group of sports bars.) In 1988, Canseco, who has admitted he'd been juicing regularly for three years at that point, smashed and slid his way to 42 homers and 40 stolen bases during his AL MVP season. Bonds matched those numbers in 1996, and did it again two years later—though the latter performance, along with A-Rod's 42/46 that same season, went almost completely unnoticed amid the Mark McGwire-Sammy Sosa duel.

A-Rod's 1998 totals stand as the greatest combination of dingers and stolen bases any player has ever posted, according to a nifty statistic called power/speed number, which Bill James introduced in 1980. The idea is simple: to show in a single figure how well a player does in both the home run and stolen base categories. Simply adding together a player's totals won't give you that, since a batter who has 60 home runs and zero stolen bases would look just as good as a player who hit 30 homers and stole 30 bases.

So here's the formula that does work:

$$\frac{(2 \times HR \times SB)}{(HR + SB)}$$

A player with no homers and 80 stolen bases will have a power/speed number of zero; 18/62 yields a P/S of 27.9; 40 taters and 40 thefts add up to a power/speed number of 40.

The all-time power/speed number rankings underscore the greatness of Rickey Henderson, Eric Davis, and, above all, Barry Bonds. Bonds has gone 30/30 five times, tying his father. And as he's aged, he's become a more selective but even better base stealer: Since 1999, Barry Bonds has stolen 61 bases and been caught stealing only 11 times, a phenomenal 85 percent success rate.

Maybe the best way to appreciate Bonds is to compare him with Luis Aparicio, a shortstop, who led the American League in stolen bases nine years in a row, from 1956 to 1964, during an 18-year Hall of Fame career. Bonds has almost as many career HR as Babe Ruth—and, going into the 2006 season, just as many stolen bases as Aparicio (506).

Now *that's* power/speed.

385.90	**386.01**	**447.05**	**490.41**	**590.19**
Joe Morgan	Bobby Bonds	Willie Mays	Rickey Henderson	Barry Bonds
268 HR	332 HR	660 HR	297 HR	708 HR
689 SB	461 SB	338 SB	1,406 SB	506 SB
No. 5	No. 4	No. 3	No. 2	No. 1

HIGHEST POWER/SPEED NUMBER, *Career*

12

HOMERS, 1 GAME

THE RECORD FOR MOST home runs in a game by both teams combined is 12, set by the White Sox and the Tigers in a crazy contest on May 28, 1995. With the wind blowing out of Tiger Stadium, Detroit's Chad Curtis ① and Cecil Fielder ② took James Baldwin deep in the bottom of the first inning. They did it again in the second. ③ ④ Then, in the top of the fourth, David Wells surrendered back-to-back-to back taters to Chicago's 7-8-9 hitters—Ray Durham, ⑤ Ron Karkovice, ⑥ and Craig Grebeck. ⑦ Two great Tigers, each playing in his final season, added three more dingers: Kirk Gibson ⑧ ⑨ socked two, Lou Whitaker ⑩ one. A homer by Frank Thomas ⑪ and another by Karkovice ⑫ brought the total for this BP-like game to an even dozen—10 of them solo shots, another record.

After each of Detroit's seven homers, loudspeakers blasted "Thus Spoke Zarathustra" (perhaps better known as the theme to *2001: A Space Odyssey*). But the White Sox overcame deficits of 7-1, 9-7, 10-9, and 11-10 to win the game, 14-12.

"It got silly after the second inning," said Tigers manager Sparky Anderson. Chicago's Tim Raines said, "Never seen anything like that in my 16 years."

Seven years later, on July 2, 2002, he could have seen 12 homers in another game—by the same two teams.

rate of home runs in the American League, which had climbed from 0.78 per game in 1992 to 0.91 in 1993 and 1.11 in 1994, hit an all-time record of 1.21.

By the late 1990s, home runs were so plentiful that the biggest single-season record of all was obviously vulnerable, and in 1998 Mark McGwire and Sammy Sosa stepped onto the national stage to take up the challenge.

They were fortunate to have each other— their friendly rivalry energized the initially reticent McGwire, charmed the nation, and kept the media heat at least somewhat dispersed.

And from a business standpoint, baseball was enormously fortunate to have both of them. McGwire and Sosa's home run barrage helped many fans get over the betrayals of MLB's recent labor wars, which had led to the cancellation of the 1994 World Series. In 1998, McGwire earned a $395,021 bonus—$1 for every fan St. Louis drew beyond 2.8 million. And the following season, although the Cardinals and Cubs were both out of contention all year, the clubs finished first and second in the NL in road attendance and both set home attendance records.

Each slugger developed a style of going deep that became famous. McGwire raised both arms in a classic gesture of triumph; Sosa clapped his hands, skipped a sideways

INNINGS										R	H	E
CHI	0	1	3	3	2	1	1	3	0	14	14	2
DET	4	3	1	1	1	1	0	1	0	12	17	1

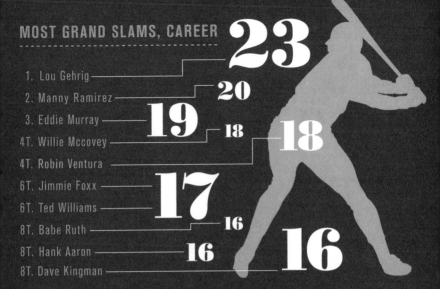

MOST GRAND SLAMS, CAREER

1. Lou Gehrig	**23**	
2. Manny Ramirez	**20**	
3. Eddie Murray	**19**	
4T. Willie Mccovey	**18**	**18**
4T. Robin Ventura		
6T. Jimmie Foxx	**17**	
6T. Ted Williams		
8T. Babe Ruth	**16**	**16**
8T. Hank Aaron	**16**	
8T. Dave Kingman		

NINE OF THE PLAYERS on this list hit 435 or more home runs apiece and rank among the game's greatest power hitters. The 10th is Robin Ventura, who is not an all-time slugger but certainly is an all-time slammer; throughout his 16 years in the big leagues, he showed an amazing knack for clearing loaded bases.

Early on, Ventura was famous for a 58-game hitting streak he put together at Oklahoma State in 1987, and for charging the mound after getting beaned by Nolan Ryan in 1993. (Ryan put him in a hilarious headlock.)

Over time, Ventura had a reputation for professionalism, Gold Glove defense at 3B, and a knack for the grand salami. On September 4, 1995, he became the first player in 25 years to hit two grand slams in one game, as the White Sox crushed Texas, 14-3. On May 20, 1999, playing for the Mets against the Brewers, he hit grand slams in both games of a doubleheader—the only player to do so.

The final slam of Ventura's career was part of a record, too: He pinch-hit a bases-loaded tater for the Dodgers on September 7, 2004, and Olmedo Saenz cracked a pinch grand slam the following night—believed to be the only time teammates have pinch-hit slams in consecutive games.

But Ventura's grandest slam of all didn't even go into the record books as a home run. It came on October 17, 1999, in the fifth game of a National League Championship Series that the Mets were trying to claw their way back into after dropping the first three games to Atlanta. The game stretched into the 15th inning, when the Braves plated a run to make the score 3-2. In the bottom of the frame, New York loaded the bases with one out against Kevin McGlinchy, the 15th pitcher. Backup catcher Todd Pratt drew a walk, tying the score. And then Ventura drove a 2-1 pitch over the right-centerfield fence.

Shea Stadium erupted in pandemonium, and as the Mets' glowing Big Apple rose out of its giant top hat beyond the outfield wall, Ventura rounded first base and was swarmed by crazed teammates. Pratt jumped into his arms and Ventura never got to second, so the official scorer credited Ventura with a single and one RBI in the 4-3 win—a big fly that became a "grand slam single" in the newspapers the next day.

Most Home Runs
by players
With the Same Name

734

Frank Thomas, 1951-1966   OF, 3B, Seven teams
Frank Thomas, 1990   1B, DH, White Sox

Ken Griffey Sr., 1973-1991   OF, Four teams
Ken Griffey Jr., 1989   OF, Mariners, Reds

688

Jose Cruz Sr., 1970-1988   OF, Cardinals, Astros, Yankees
Jose Cruz Jr., 1997   OF, Seven teams

358

Bob Johnson, 1933-1945   OF, A's, Senators, Red Sox
Bob Johnson, 1960-1970   IF, Seven teams
Bob Johnson, 1969-1977   P, Five teams
Bob Johnson, 1981-1983   C, Rangers

341

Luis Gonzalez, 1990   OF, Four teams
Luis A. Gonzalez, 2004   2B, Rockies

337

Reggie Sanders, 1974   1B, Tigers
Reggie Sanders, 1991   OF, Seven teams

295

Gary Matthews Sr., 1972-1987   OF, Five teams
Gary Matthews Jr., 1999   OF, Seven teams

293

Earl Averill Sr., 1929-1941   OF, Indians, Tigers, Braves
Earl Averill Jr., 1956-1963   C, Five teams

282

Bernie Williams, 1970-1974   OF, Giants, Padres
Bernie Williams, 1991   OF, Yankees

279

Joe Morgan, 1959-1964   3B, Five teams
Joe Morgan, 1963-1984   2B, Five teams

270

step toward first, and trotted around the bases, then pounded his heart with his fist and offered a two-fingered kiss and a V sign to fans. And they wrapped up their joint pursuit of the single-season record in dramatic fashion.

Throughout the summer of 1998, Big Mac took leads on Sosa, only to have Sammy pull within reach. But McGwire passed Maris first, going yard off Steve Trachsel of Sosa's Cubs on September 8 for his 62nd home run. (At 341 feet, it was McGwire's shortest shot of the year.) Sosa jogged over to congratulate McGwire, and the two men bear-hugged.

Sosa caught McGwire at 62 and 65, and after hitting his 66th dinger on September 25, a massive blast at the Astrodome, Sosa took sole possession of first place in the NL home run chase. He held it 45 minutes. McGwire homered that day and four more times in his final two games, to finish the season with 70.

CONSECUTIVE GAME HOMERS

ON JULY 28, 1993, Seattle's Ken Griffey Jr. homered off the Twins' Willie Banks, giving him dingers in eight straight games to tie a major-league record jointly held by Dale Long of the Pirates (May 1956) and Don Mattingly of the Yankees (July 1987).

THE HOME RUN CYCLE

ON JULY 27, 1998, Tyrone Horne of the Arkansas Travelers became the only player in the history of organized baseball to hit for the "home run cycle."

In a Texas League game at San Antonio, Horne blasted a two-run homer out of Nelson Wolff Stadium in the first inning, then followed with a grand slam in the second, and a solo shot in the fifth, all off Missions starter Peter Zamora. In the sixth, he knocked a three-run dinger off Miguel Garcia, finishing the night with four home runs—one of each type. Horne had 37 HR and 139 RBI that season, but the minor-league outfielder never made it to the majors.

CLEARING BASES, NOT FENCES

IN THE FINAL GAME of the 1999 season, Randy Winn of the Devil Rays became the most recent player to hit an inside-the-park grand slam. Winn's drive to left-centerfield helped last-place Tampa Bay to a 6-2 win over the Yankees, who had already clinched home-field advantage in the AL playoffs and were resting most of their regulars.

Inside-the-park slams are uncommon, but not as rare as you might think: There have been five since 1991.

The 1998 race was fun, exhilarating, and—at the time, anyway—restorative. After it was over, McGwire said, "I'm, like, in awe of myself." He predicted his new record wouldn't be broken for some time.

He was wrong.

Make no mistake: The home run had arrived as a cultural force. In the spring of 1999, Nike debuted an ad featuring Greg Maddux and Tom Glavine, envious of McGwire, practicing their power strokes and thereby catching the attention of Heather Locklear. "Chicks dig the long ball" was more than an instant classic; as Howard Bryant wrote, "The sport that could never properly market itself had finally found a marketable star: the home run."

But unlike Babe Ruth in 1927 or Maris in 1961, who each

TONY LAZZERI, YANKEES	MAY 24, 1936
JIM TABOR, RED SOX	JULY 4, 1939
RUDY YORK, RED SOX	JULY 27, 1946
TONY CLONINGER, BRAVES	JULY 3, 1966
JIM NORTHRUP, TIGERS	JUNE 24, 1968
FRANK ROBINSON, ORIOLES	JUNE 26, 1970
ROBIN VENTURA, WHITE SOX	SEPTEMBER 4, 1995
FERNANDO TATIS, CARDINALS	**APRIL 23, 1999**
NOMAR GARCIAPARRA, RED SOX	MAY 10, 1999
BILL MUELLER, RED SOX	JULY 29, 2003

TWO GRAND SLAMS IN ONE GAME

FERNANDO TATIS IS the only man who needed enough mustard to cover two grand salamis in the same inning. In Los Angeles on April 23, 1999, the Cards third baseman clocked Chan Ho Park twice in the third with the bases loaded—once with no outs and again with two outs.

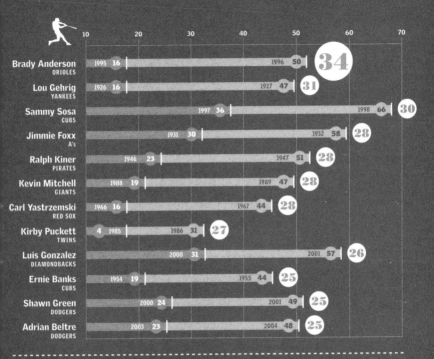

	10	20	30	40	50	60	70

Brady Anderson ORIOLES — 1995 16 — 1996 50 — **34**

Lou Gehrig YANKEES — 1926 16 — 1927 47 — **31**

Sammy Sosa CUBS — 1997 36 — 1998 66 — **30**

Jimmie Foxx A's — 1931 30 — 1932 58 — **28**

Ralph Kiner PIRATES — 1946 23 — 1947 51 — **28**

Kevin Mitchell GIANTS — 1988 19 — 1989 47 — **28**

Carl Yastrzemski RED SOX — 1966 16 — 1967 44 — **28**

Kirby Puckett TWINS — 4 1985 — 1986 31 — **27**

Luis Gonzalez DIAMONDBACKS — 2000 31 — 2001 57 — **26**

Ernie Banks CUBS — 1954 19 — 1955 44 — **25**

Shawn Green DODGERS — 2000 24 — 2001 49 — **25**

Adrian Beltre DODGERS — 2003 23 — 2004 48 — **25**

BIGGEST
ONE-YEAR JUMP IN
HOME RUNS

Brady Anderson's home run jump in 1995–1996 is not only the biggest of all time, but also one of the biggest flukes. Many of the players on this list were budding but genuine sluggers who showed dramatic increases in power as they developed or moved into better hitting conditions. As a group, they averaged 21.4 homers in the first year listed and 49.3 in the second, and then regressed to 33.3 in the following season. That means that overall, they kept about 43 percent of their home run surge. But Anderson kept just 5 percent of his dinger jump, while Gonzalez and Beltre fell back below where they had started.

"This is the type of thing that as a kid you dream about."

GOOD GRIEF!

-Scott Brosius

Yankees 3B, on hitting the game-winning homer
in Game 3 of the 1998 World Series

CHARLIE BROWN, pitcher-manager for a team that at one point had a record of 2–930, was the most famous as well as the most futile Little Leaguer in the country from the time *Peanuts* debuted in 1950 until Charles M. Schulz' retirement in 1999. But Charlie Brown's moment in the sun finally came on March 30, 1993, when he hit a home run in the ninth inning, his team won the game, and he was the hero.

His sister Sally, of course, responded, "You?!"

nudged the single-season record by a single digit to a mark that wouldn't be touched for decades, McGwire's 1998 performance signaled a dramatic change in the supply, and thus the value, of home runs.

Inside the game, dingers were coming cheap.

Feats that had been extraordinarily rare, such as going deep four times in a game or smacking 30 homers by the All-Star break, became much more common in this era. And so did passing the previously magical mark of 60 home runs a season. McGwire hit 65 and Sosa 63 in 1999, and Sosa followed up with 64 in 2001—the year the nation offered a rather blasé reaction to Barry Bonds raising the bar to 73 homers.

In the spring of 2000, while a staggering 44 batters were on their way to hitting 30 or more home runs apiece, Associated Press reporter Jim Litke called Bud Selig at home and asked if he was worried that balls might be flying out of parks for unnatural reasons.

"Let's just see how this plays out," Selig said, revealing his fundamental strategy. "Of course, we have concerns," he added. "But at this stage, we're just sitting back and monitoring."

The truth was that by then, major league baseball was in the throes of an addiction to weight training and had been for some time. And the best evidence available today indicates that if factors other than conditioning, often enhanced by anabolic supplements and steroids, contributed to the 1990s home run boom, they did so only in a minor way.

Consider ballparks. In the 1990s, franchises began turning away from the designs of the 1960s, 1970s, and 1980s and started building baseball-only stadiums, sometimes fitting them into downtown business districts. Camden Yards led the way, and several of the

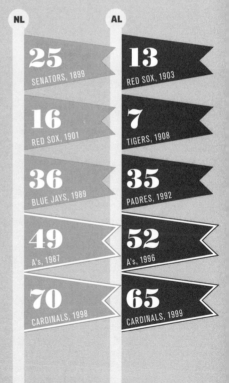

PLAYERS WHO HAVE LED BOTH AL AND NL IN HOME RUNS

	NL	AL
BUCK FREEMAN	25 SENATORS, 1899	13 RED SOX, 1903
SAM CRAWFORD	16 RED SOX, 1901	7 TIGERS, 1908
FRED McGRIFF	36 BLUE JAYS, 1989	35 PADRES, 1992
MARK McGWIRE	49 A's, 1987	52 A's, 1996
	70 CARDINALS, 1998	65 CARDINALS, 1999

IN ADDITION TO LEADING each league in dingers twice, something no other player has done, Mark McGwire is also the only player to lead the majors in home runs without leading either league. In 1997, he hit 34 homers for Oakland, then 24 more after being traded to St. Louis on July 31, for a total of 58—more than AL champ Ken Griffey Jr. (56) or NL leader Larry Walker (49).

MOST HOME RUNS BY A TEAM, SEASON

1.	Mariners, 1997	264
2.	Rangers, 2005	260
3.	Orioles, 1996	257
4.	Astros, 2000	249
5.	Rangers, 2001	246
6.	Mariners, 1996	245
7T.	Mariners, 1999	244
7T.	Blue Jays, 2000	244
9.	Athletics, 1996	243
10T.	White Sox, 2004	242
10T.	Yankees, 2004	242

parks that followed had cozy dimensions and relatively little foul territory. Coors Field (which opened in 1995), the Ballpark in Arlington (1994), Great American Ballpark (2003), and Citizens Bank Park (2004) are among the best power hitters' parks in baseball, so it's natural to assume that trends in architecture helped send dinger totals soaring. But Comerica Park, opened in 2000, is a terrible stadium for sluggers, as are Pac Bell Park (2000) and Petco Park (2004).

"Intuitively, I believed that most of the increase in home runs was from bringing into baseball the new parks," says Bill James. "But when I actually studied the issue—not true. Actually, there were almost as many pitcher's parks added in that era as hitter's parks, and the increase in home runs in the parks

The $3,000,000 HOME RUN BALL

SEPTEMBER 27, 1998: Mark McGwire smacks his 70th and final home run of a legendary season, connecting in the seventh inning off Carl Pavano of the Expos. The ball rockets off McGwire's bat, bangs off the leftfield bleachers at Busch Stadium, and bounces into the Washington University luxury box. Philip Ozersky, a 26-year-old scientist who makes $30,000 a year helping to map the human genome, drops his beer, dives for the ball, and comes up with it. It's the first home run ball he's ever retrieved, and he wants to show it to his family. But security men rush Ozersky away and take him to a room where

the Cardinals officials offer him autographed memorabilia and a meeting with McGwire in exchange for the ball. He declines.

DECEMBER 8, 1998: Guernsey's, a New York auction house, announces that it will sell seven balls from the 1998 home run race: McGwire's 70th, 68th, 67th, and 63rd; and Sammy Sosa's 66th, 64th, and 61st. Mike Barnes, a 28-year-old lawyer representing the owners of six of the balls (the Cubs own the seventh), says Ozersky has already received written offers of more than $1 million for McGwire's 70th.

"I would have loved to keep the ball, but I was concerned about the tax implications if

[that did not change] was comparable to the overall increase." James calculates that only about 20 percent of the boom in home runs can be attributed to ballparks.

Balls can't be blamed, either. In 2000, MLB commissioned a study at the University of Massachusetts Lowell, in which a couple of hundred baseballs were subjected to various measurements and stresses. The team that examined the balls reported their tests "revealed no significant performance differences." Batches of baseballs can vary a bit in their tendency to rebound when hit, but balls were manufactured in the 1990s the same way they always were.

The strike zone? The de facto strike zone—the area generally called a strike by umpires, whatever the rules—

MOST HOME RUNS ALLOWED BY A TEAM, SEASON

1.	Tigers, 1996	241
2.	Royals, 2000	239
2T.	Rockies, 2001	239
4.	Rockies, 1999	237
5.	Reds, 2004	236
6.	Astros, 2000	234
7.	Twins, 1996	233
8.	Cubs, 2000	231
9.	Angels, 2000	228
10.	Orioles, 1987	228

I kept it or gave it away," Ozersky says later. "I came to the conclusion that the greater good would be served if I used the ball to help myself and the people around me."

Ozerksy, who isn't married, says he plans to invest some of his proceeds, give some to his parents, and donate some to the American Cancer Society, Cardinals Care (the team's community foundation), and the Leukemia Society of America.

JANUARY 12, 1999: Ozersky's ball—stamped with a number, brushed with a one-of-a-kind DNA sample for identification purposes, and inscribed in invisible ink—goes on sale at the theater at Madison Square Garden. "I hope it goes below a million," says Scott Goodman, a collector who had been part of a group trying to buy the ball from Ozersky. The auction opens at $500,000, and dozens of bidders quickly push the price past $1 million, then $2 million, at which point the audience erupts into

applause. Participating by phone, Todd McFarlane, creator of Spawn, ultimately gets the ball with a bid of $2.7 million. (Adding a 15 percent commission for the auction house, the purchase price is $3.1 million.)

"We don't have royalty," said Marshall Fishwick, a communications professor at Virginia Tech, in 1999, in words that ring as true today as they did then. "We don't have relics. So these items become our relics, our precious objects. That home run race was the one great event of 1998 that was positive ... Maybe we can't handle Iraq, but, by God, we can hit home runs."

The winning bid for McGwire's 70th dwarfed prices for other historic home run balls. Sosa's 66th, which also went to McFarlane at the Guernsey's auction, sold for $150,000. Before that, the record had been $126,500 for the first home run ball in Yankee Stadium, hit by Babe Ruth in 1923. And nothing since has come close.

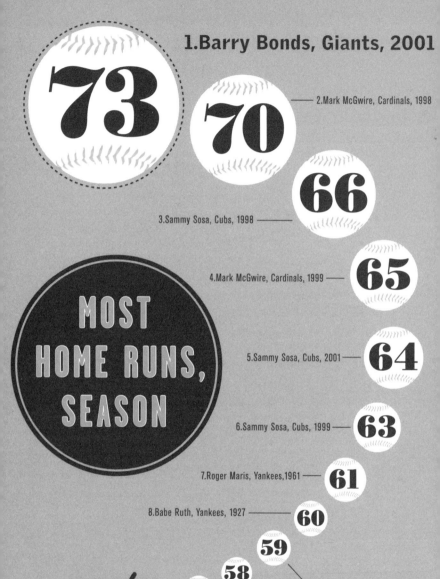

73 1.Barry Bonds, Giants, 2001

70 2.Mark McGwire, Cardinals, 1998

66 3.Sammy Sosa, Cubs, 1998

65 4.Mark McGwire, Cardinals, 1999

MOST
HOME RUNS,
SEASON

64 5.Sammy Sosa, Cubs, 2001

63 6.Sammy Sosa, Cubs, 1999

7.Roger Maris, Yankees,1961 **61**

8.Babe Ruth, Yankees, 1927 **60**

59

58

58 **58**

9.Babe Ruth, Yankees,1921

10T.Jimmie Foxx, A's, 1932

10T.Hank Greenberg, Tigers, 1938

10T.Mark McGwire, A's/ Cardinals, 1997

> "I'm always amazed when a pitcher becomes angry at a hitter for hitting a home run. When I strike out, I don't get angry at the pitcher, I get angry at myself."
>
> *- Willie Stargell*

MOST PINCH HIT HOME RUNS, SEASON

7	Dave Hansen 2000 DODGERS
7	Craig Wilson 2001 PIRATES
6	Johnny Frederick 1932 DODGERS

shrank throughout the 1970s and 1980s. Eventually, MLB redefined the official strike zone in 1988 and 1996 to help pitchers. But home runs kept increasing anyway.

No, it seems that the bulk of the rise in power came from bulk itself—from players' increasing willingness to do whatever it took to add pounds of muscle. The Oakland A's began a bigger-is-better movement in the late 1980s, and some of their sluggers took weight training to extremes. Jose Canseco began juicing as a minor leaguer in Huntsville, Alabama, and when he got to the Show, he started working out with Curtis Wenzlaff, an advocate of extreme training who taped weights to his hands and sometimes slept in a sensory-deprivation tank—and who used an array of high-powered steroids. As first reported in 2005 in the *New York Daily News*, Wenzlaff took on McGwire as a customer as well, supplying him with testosterone, Winstrol V, and a veterinary steroid called Equipoise. By 1991, Wenzlaff was jetting around the country to supply more than 20 to 30 major-league ballplayers, hiding the steroids he carried by wrapping them in tin foil and putting them inside shoes in his luggage.

For a long while, the commissioner's office was oblivious to the spread of anabolic steroids throughout baseball. Selig was a big fan of the Milwaukee Braves in the 1950s; his image of a power hitter was the young Hank Aaron, not a muscle-bound weightlifter. And to the extent that most baseball executives thought about fighting drug use, they mostly wanted testing to police cocaine, the game's problem drug in the 1980s.

Over time, however, their ignorance became willful. MLB officials shrugged off information from an FBI agent about Canseco and Wenzlaff. When team doctors, concerned about the new injuries they were seeing, asked to distribute

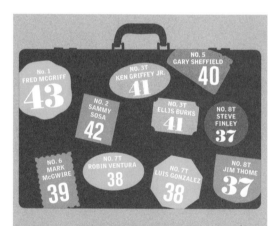

MOST BALLPARKS HOMERED IN, CAREER

FRED MCGRIFF didn't make it to 500 home runs, but he did reach the top of this list. The final dinger of his 19-year career came on June 17, 2004, at Petco Park in San Diego, the 43rd stadium from which he launched at least one home run.

WHAT'S THE FREQUENCY, BARRY?

HIGHEST % HOME RUNS PER AT-BAT, *Season*

BARRY BONDS 2001 Giants (73 HR/476 AB)	15.34
SHANE SPENCER 1998 Yankees (10 HR/67 AB)	14.93
TED WILLIAMS 1953 Red Sox (13 HR/91 AB)	14.29
MARK McGWIRE 1998 Cardinals (70 HR/509 AB)	13.75
MARK McGWIRE 2000 Cardinals (32 HR/236 AB)	13.56
MARK McGWIRE 1999 Cardinals (65 HR/521 AB)	12.49
MARK McGWIRE 1995 A's (39 HR/317 AB)	12.30
MARK McGWIRE 1996 A's (52 HR/423 AB)	12.29
BARRY BONDS 2004 Giants (45 HR/373 AB)	12.06
BABE RUTH 1920 Yankees (54 HR/457 AB)	11.92

HIGHEST % HOME RUNS PER AT-BAT, *Career*

MARK McGWIRE (583 HR/6,187 AB)	9.42
BABE RUTH (714 HR/8,397 AB)	8.50
BARRY BONDS (708 HR/9,140 AB)	7.75
JIM THOME (430 HR/5,919 AB)	7.26
MANNY RAMIREZ (435 HR/5,919 AB)	7.10
RALPH KINER (435 HR/6,126 AB)	7.09
HARMON KILLEBREW (573 HR/8,147 AB)	7.03
SAMMY SOSA (588 HR/8,401 AB)	7.00
ADAM DUNN (158 HR/2,271 AB)	6.96
ALEX RODRIGUEZ (429 HR/6,195 AB)	6.92

SIGN OF THE TIMES

THE NL RECORD for home runs in a season by a DH: four, by Jim Thome in 2004.

information to players about the effects of steroids and "nutritional" supplements, it took Selig and the players' union several years to say yes. And when the news broke in August 1998 that McGwire was using androstenedione, a then-legal anabolic supplement, the commissioner immediately supported the superstar.

McGwire's admission that he was using andro should have led baseball and the sportswriters who cover it to wonder what else he was on, and to find out what substances other players were ingesting. Instead, the story got buried. "This Persecution of McGwire a Crime" was the title of an August column by the *Boston Globe*'s Dan Shaughnessy, which incorrectly claimed that "'andro' is an all-natural, over-the-counter steroid (not of the dangerous anabolic steroid family)." When McGwire hit his 62nd home run, Mike Bianchi of the *Florida Times-Union* called the Cardinals' slugger a "red-haired, freckle-faced jolly good giant." Bianchi wrote, "I don't want to hear anything about that Andro-whatchamacallit today. No way. Don't even bring it up."

As anabolics spread throughout baseball in the 1990s, they distorted the traditional balance between hitters and pitchers, leading some pitchers to juice to keep pace and forcing clean players into excruciating decisions about how to keep their lineup or roster spots. Minor leaguers and players at younger levels felt that pressure, too. And here's something else to keep in mind that most fans still don't realize: Throughout this era, taking steroids was against baseball's rules, whether or not MLB had effective drug testing (or any testing at all). Commissioner Fay Vincent explicitly banned the use of illegal steroids in a 1991 memo that he sent to all teams and the union. And

MOST HOME RUNS BY TWO TEAMMATES, SEASON

No. 2
2001, GIANTS
BARRY BONDS 73
RICH AURILIA 37
110

No. 1
1961, YANKEES
ROGER MARIS 61
MICKEY MANTLE 54
115

No. 3
1927, YANKEES
BABE RUTH 60
LOU GEHRIG 47
107

No. 4
1998, CARDINALS
MARK MCGWIRE 70
RAY LANKFORD 31
101

No. 6T
1999, CARDINALS
MARK MCGWIRE 65
FERNANDO TATIS 34
99

No. 5
2002, RANGERS
ALEX RODRIGUEZ 57
RAFAEL PALMEIRO 43
100

No. 6T
2001, RANGERS
ALEX RODRIGUEZ 52
RAFAEL PALMEIRO 47
99

No. 9
1998, CUBS
SAMMY SOSA 66
HENRY RODRIGUEZ 31
97

No. 8
1997, MARINERS
KEN GRIFFEY 56
ALEX RODRIGUEZ 42
98

No. 10T
1997, MARINERS
KEN GRIFFEY JR. 56
JAY BUHNER 40
96

No. 10T
1998, CARDINALS
MARK MCGWIRE 70
RON GANT 26
96

YOU WANNA PLAY HARDBALL?

A GUY HITS A home run, the next guy up better be ready to go down. It's been that way in baseball since Abner Doubleday didn't invent the game in the 19th century.

Since the beginning of divisional play in 1969, two pitchers are tied for the major-league lead in Drilled Batters Immediately Following a Home Run, with eight DBIFHRs each. One you probably expect: Randy Johnson. The other you almost certainly don't: Danny Darwin.

Darwin was a cantankerous sort; he had an ominous nickname (Dr. Death) and he was around forever (21 seasons), which gave him plenty of payback ops. But with only .25 batters hit per HR allowed, he was still a far less likely candidate to pick up a DBIFHR than Johnson, who in 18 seasons has nailed .50 batters for every HR allowed.

Look for the Big Unit to pass Dr. Death some time in 2006.

"I don't think Hank's home run record will ever be broken. There's no way."

–David Justice

though he surely has been slow to acknowledge how long it's been around, Selig reiterated the policy in a 1997 document.

Just something to keep in mind when you decide how to look back at the players and stats of an era flush with home run fever.

In September 1998, *Science World* published a brief article on McGwire's physique. In a typical at-bat, the piece explained, McGwire's back foot would push his frame forward about 18 inches, giving his body kinetic energy, and as he stepped into a pitch, the rotation of his hips and body toward the pitcher's mound would add more energy. In the last 20th-second of his swing, he would stop stepping and twisting, and all his energy would transfer to his bat, which he would whip around at a speed of 70 to 75 miles per hour—10 miles per hour faster than an average player.

`"McGwire's brawn lets him pump more energy into his swing than the average player," the story said, and more energy led to greater distances for batted balls.

Three years later, shortly after Bonds broke his home run record, McGwire, suffering from back and knee injuries, tried to play in the 2001 postseason. He had hit .187 that year, and proceeded to go one for 11 in St. Louis' series against Arizona before his turn came to bat in the ninth inning of the fifth and final game. There was a runner on first with nobody out.

Manager Tony La Russa lifted McGwire for a pinch-hitter, who bunted.

McGwire never played again. Patellar tendonitis, a painful inflammation of the piece of the body that connects the kneecap to the shin, helped do him in. It's a fairly common problem in athletes who tend to jump around excessively, like volleyball players. In someone who doesn't move around a lot, it's probably a sign that a person's body has become so huge that it's literally ripping away from his frame.

Baseball doctors say they didn't see this kind of injury much before the mid-1990s.

MOST HOME RUNS BY THE ALL-STAR BREAK

39 BARRY BONDS, 2001 Giants

37 REGGIE JACKSON 1969 A's
MARK McGWIRE, 1998 Cardinals

35 LUIS GONZALEZ, 2001 Diamondbacks
KEN GRIFFEY JR. 1998 Mariners

34 FRANK HOWARD, 1969 Senators

33 KEN GRIFFEY JR., 1994 Mariners
ROGER MARIS, 1961 Yankees
MARK McGWIRE, 1987 A's
SAMMY SOSA, 1998 Cubs
MATT WILLIAMS, 1994 Giants

The greatest player anyone reading these pages is likely to see, Barry Bonds is also one of baseball's most reviled superstars.

WITH A COMBINATION OF POWER and plate discipline unmatched at least since Ted Williams, Bonds holds the single-season home run record (73 in 2001) and, with 708 career dingers, opened the 2006 season in hot pursuit of Babe Ruth (714) and Hank Aaron (755). But throughout a career that has netted him an otherworldly seven MVP awards, Bonds has remained unapologetically uninterested in cultivating the affections of teammates, sportswriters or fans.

He has also been a long-term, heavy user of performance-enhancing drugs, according to published reports that broke in March 2006.

You know about Bonds' personality. Tagging him as arrogant doesn't do justice to the way he has leveraged his immense talent into creating his own world within a team sport. Bonds has considerable charm and intelligence, but he came into baseball pre-programmed by his father, Bobby, and his godfather, Willie Mays, to expect the worst from outsiders, and has spent 20 years churlishly walling himself off from the rest of us.

As a player, Bonds continues to be, of course, the central character in baseball's steroids drama. He first tried andro in January 1997, according to research by my ESPN The Magazine colleague Shaun Assael. And according to Mark Fainaru-Wada and Lance Williams of the San Francisco Chronicle, Bonds turned to harder stuff as he watched the 1998 home run derby. Among the substances Bonds allegedly used: Clomid, a women's fertility drug; human growth hormone; insulin; modafinil, a narcolepsy treatment; trenbolone, a steroid used to bulk up cattle; and "the cream" and "the clear," designer anabolics from BALCO laboratories.

The exposure of Bonds' reported juicing gravely threatens his legacy, which has two parts. Through the 2000 season, Bonds' career traced a comprehensible path. He had won the last of his three MVP awards seven years earlier. He had last led the league in OPS in 1995. He still had immense power, but was losing some of his speed, and had lost a third of a season to injuries in 1999. All of this suggests an arc with an extremely high peak, but one that is still parabolic.

Bonds' back-to-back MVP awards in 1992

BARRY BONDS

BARRY BONDS STATS

Year	Team	G	R	HR	RBI	BB	AVG	OPS
1986	Pirates	113	72	16	48	65	.223	.746
1987	Pirates	150	99	25	59	54	.261	.821
1988	Pirates	144	97	24	58	72	.283	.859
1989	Pirates	159	96	19	58	93	.248	.777
1990	Pirates	151	104	33	114	93	.301	.970
1991	Pirates	153	95	25	116	107	.292	.924
1992	Pirates	140	109	34	103	127	.311	1.080
1993	Giants	159	129	46	123	126	.336	1.136
1994	Giants	112	89	37	81	74	.312	1.073
1995	Giants	144	109	33	104	120	.294	1.009
1996	Giants	158	122	42	129	151	.308	1.076
1997	Giants	159	123	40	101	145	.291	1.031
1998	Giants	156	120	37	122	130	.303	1.047
1999	Giants	102	91	34	83	73	.262	1.006
2000	Giants	143	129	49	106	117	.306	1.127
2001	Giants	153	129	73	137	177	.328	1.379
2002	Giants	143	117	46	110	198	.370	1.381
2003	Giants	130	111	45	90	148	.341	1.278
2004	Giants	147	129	45	101	232	.362	1.422
2005	Giants	14	8	5	10	9	.286	1.071
	Career Totals	2730	2078	708	1853	2311	.300	1.053

and 1993 represent a level reached by very few players, with the latter season, his first in San Francisco, ranking among the very greatest ever put together by a left fielder. Playing half his games in Candlestick Park, under terrible hitting conditions, Bonds smacked 46 homers and posted an OPS of 1.136, the highest in baseball since Norm Cash in 1961. Essentially, through the first 2,000 games of his career, Bonds showed that at his peak, he could hit like Williams while stealing up to 52 bases a year and perennially winning Gold Gloves.

But then he slugged 73 home runs in 2001. And hit .370 to win a batting title in 2002. And drew 232 walks, 120 of them intentional, in 2004. Those numbers are

beyond incredible—and they changed not only the shape of Bonds' career, and not only the games in which he appeared (often reducing them to spectacles staged around his plate appearances), but also the very fabric of baseball's statistical history.

The single least understood aspect of baseball stats is this: everything is relative not to league averages but to the gap between league leaders and league averages. It's easiest to see this with batting averages. In 1925, Rogers Hornsby, then with the Cardinals, hit .403. He was able to do so not only because it was a great year for National League batters overall—the entire league batted .292—but because in those days, dominant players could exceed run-of-the-

...him performers to an exceptional extent.

In 1908, Honus Wagner hit .354, 48% better than the National League average of .239. Hornsby exceeded the league in 1925 by 38%. By 1991, Terry Pendleton was winning the NL batting title with a .319 mark, just 28% better than the league (.250).

This gap, across almost all categories, has been shrinking through most of baseball history, with the exception of periods (such as World War II or just after expansions) when subpar players have entered the game, allowing league leaders to temporarily establish greater dominance.

Stephen Jay Gould explained why in 1986: as the average talent level of all players rises, it becomes harder for exceptional players to truly stand out. Back when Wee Willie Keeler said, "Hit 'em where they ain't," Gould wrote, it was easier for players to take his advice. But with bigger, stronger, more racially diverse players, nobody could tower over the game the way Babe Ruth did.

Until Barry Bonds.

Bonds singlehandedly jammed the decline in the gap between league leaders and league averages, and then threw it into reverse. For instance, with slugging averages of .863 in 2001 (103% better than the NL average) and .812 in 2004 (92% better), Bonds surpassed his peers to a Ruthian degree, when by all rights the undertow of the modern, global talent pool should have been dragging him back to the pack.

And so the question of how much illegal performance enhancers contributed to Bonds' performance isn't just disturbing, it is key to fully evaluating him. Bonds' first 15 seasons

make him one of the three best left fielders i... history; his next four would make him one o... the three best players in history. Too bad w... can no longer take them seriously.

We will probably never know the entir... story of what Bonds was ingesting and when—MLB allowed its version of Dealey Plaza to go virtually uninvestigated. Bu... we can examine what his career might have... looked like if he had available to him only the... strength and conditioning techniques used by comparable sluggers of the past.

Suppose we examine the 16 players who hit 500 home runs and are not currently active, and see how their performance changed from season to season as they grew older. For example, this group averaged 83 RBI at the age of 38 and 76, 8.4% fewer, at age 39. If we do this for every category in every year, we'll come up with a composite profile of how history's greatest sluggers aged. Then apply that profile to Bonds, taking his career stats through age 35 and grafting onto them a historically typical decline due to age instead of the numbers he actually posted.

At the bottom of the page you'll see what Bonds' career might look like if he had aged the way other great power hitters did instead of exploding in 2001. Basically, had he stayed clean, he could have been Willie Mays with better plate discipline.

If the reports about Bonds are correct, cheating helped net him a 73-dinger season and a $90-million contract. But now fans will likely disdain his entire career, not merely the portion of it amped by the juice.

Who will care about what he could have been?

	G	AB	R	H	HR	RBI	BB	SO	AVG
THROUGH AGE 35	2143	7456	1584	2157	494	1405	1547	1189	.28...
ACTUAL, THROUGH 2005	2730	9140	2078	2742	708	1853	2311	1434	.30...
ADJUSTED, THROUGH 2005	2686	9225	1987	2656	634	1780	1921	1496	.28...

ALBERT PUJOLS

CHAPTER 7

2005–

★ ★ ★

Deflation?

It's clear how Commissioner Bud Selig

would like this final chapter to go: with me reporting that Major League
Baseball and the Major League Baseball Players Association agreed to a
tough new drug policy on January 13, 2005, and thereby cleaned up the
game. No more juice, no more hairy-backed, acne-covered 'roid freaks
perverting the national pastime! For evidence, just look at the numbers:
home runs and total runs down, complete games and shutouts up.

1876–1919 1920–1945 1946–1962 1963–1976 1977–1992 1983–2004 2005–

A HIT, A HOME RUN, MAYBE A WIN

ON AUGUST 23, 2005,
Jacque Jones hit a home
run off the White Sox'
Freddy Garcia, which was
enough for Minnesota to
beat Chicago, 1-0, even
though that dinger was the
only hit Garcia allowed.

One-hitters where the
sole hit is a homer occur,
on average, about once
a season. And on the 10
occasions it's happened
since 1995, the one-hit team,
including Jones' Twins, has
won the game four times.

And in fact, that's the story

many sportswriters were willing to tell in the 2005 season. On May 30, *Sports Illustrated* ran a cover with the headline, "The Incredible Shrinking Slugger." Inside, a story called "When Bigger Gets Smaller, Small Gets Big" addressed the implications of baseball's new drug policy: "Did you just feel that? ... [I]t looks as though 2005 will provide another one of history's hairpin turns ... Isn't it logical to expect that as the game moved from no steroids policy to one with public sanctions, there would have to be some effect on how the game is played?"

Well, it might be logical to expect so, but not to conclude as much. At least not yet. In 2005, major league players clubbed 5,017 homers. That's down 9 percent from the previous year and 11 percent from 2000, but it's well within the season-to-season fluctuations baseball has seen over the years. By itself, last year's drop wasn't meaningful.

It's true that Selig got the players to crack open their collective bargaining agreement in the winter of 2004–05 and hike penalties for failed drug tests. And after a particularly disastrous performance by baseball personnel on Capitol Hill in March—the one where Mark McGwire, shrunk to the size of a teabag, wouldn't answer questions about his past—the commissioner decided to break with the union.

Selig put the union in the hot seat by demanding even stiffer penalties, culminating with a lifetime ban for a third failed test and testing for amphetamines. And by the middle of November, he had almost everything he wanted.

Now, there are at least three reasons why home runs might

CONTINUED ON PAGE 178

No. 1
ALEX RODRIGUEZ
281

No. 2
BARRY BONDS
263

No. 3
SAMMY SOSA
252

No. 4
MANNY RAMIREZ
237

No. 5
JIM THOME
234

No. 6
ANDRUW JONES
221

No. 7
CARLOS DELGADO
220

No. 8T
GARY SHEFFIELD
213

No. 8T
VLADIMIR GUERRERO
213

No. 10
JIM EDMONDS
210

MOST HOME RUNS
2000 2005

MOST CAREER HOME RUNS,
BY POSITION

LINE-UP CARD

566

345

1B	A	Mark McGwire	R
	B		
2B	A	Jeff Kent	R
	B		
SS	A	Cal Ripken Jr.	R
	B		
3B	A	Mike Schmidt	R
	B		
OF	A	Barry Bonds	L
	B		
C	A	Mike Piazza	R
	B		
DH	A	Edgar Martinez	R
	B	~~Harold Baines~~	
P	A	Wes Ferrell	R
	B		

306

FIVE HALL OF FAMERS, a DH, a pitcher—and Jeff Kent. Kent has slugged over .500 in a career that's going to pass 2,000 games in 2006. But he doesn't feel like a Hall of Famer to a lot of people. He is (at best) an average fielder, he has played in an era of inflated stats, and he a difficult personality (read: unpopular among baseball writers who vote for the HOF). His career will be a test case of how much Cooperstown—actually, the Baseball Writers Association of America—values raw home run totals.

509

697

376

225

37

keep dropping toward more historically normal levels. First, while MLB's new policy still has holes—it's not clear how players will be tested in the off-season, for example, or how baseball plans to police the use of human growth hormone—its harsh penalties still may serve as a deterrent to juicing.

Woefully short on education and overlapping incompletely with the World Anti-Doping Agency's list of banned substances, MLB's anti-drug initiative is hard for many players to understand, but it may well be easy for them to fear.

Second, the minor league players have been subject to random drug tests for years, and it's reasonable to think that players who have arrived in the big leagues recently are less prone to steroid use.

Third, because pitching talent seemed so scarce in the high-scoring 1990s and early 2000s, teams put a premium on developing it. While many of the game's biggest power hitters, from Barry Bonds to Ken Griffey Jr. to Sammy Sosa, are winding down their careers, lots of great young pitchers are in the pipeline. Think of Dontrelle Willis, Ben Sheets, and Rich Harden.

CLUTCH HOME RUN HITTERS

SINCE 1993, 72 players have hit at least 200 dingers. Of all the home runs clouted by those hitters—20,989, to be precise—41.6 percent either tied games or put their teams ahead. At first glance, the figures for individual sluggers seem to be all over the map: Mark McGwire (47.4 percent) and Barry Bonds (45.7 percent) are well above average, while Sammy Sosa (40.3 percent) is sub par, and Paul Konerko (34.3 percent) ranks dead last.

But upon closer examination, most of the variation in these statistics can just be chalked up to luck. In only two cases is a player's "clutch" average more than two standard deviations beyond the mean—that is, the chance of his performance being a fluke is roughly 5 percent. **Craig Biggio's** home runs tied games or put his team ahead 53 percent of the time, as did 51.1 percent of **Gary Sheffield's** homers. By this method, Biggio and Sheffield are the true clutch home run hitters of today.

If you had to hazard a guess about where baseball's homers might be heading, it would probably be safest to predict a continued but moderate decline. The game may well be headed for boutique cheating, where most players will be deterred from using illegal drugs, but others who are both smart and super-rich may hire private performance consultants to custom-supply them with impossible-to-detect substances—the way BALCO used to do.

But the cat-and-mice games that hitters, pitchers, and testers play are complicated, and it's just too early yet to say where dingers will level off.

Amid all the anabolic controversies involving McGwire, Jose Canseco, and Rafael Palmeiro, 2005 saw its share of memorable dingers. Dmitri Young hit three homers in a game on Opening Day. Jeremy Hermida became the first player to hit a grand slam in his first major-league at-bat since Bill Duggleby in 1898. Manny Ramirez bashed the 20th grand slam of his career; he now ranks second on the all-time list behind Lou Gehrig (23).

And then on October 17, we were served up a hum-dinger.

St. Louis trailed Houston three games to one in the National League Championship Series, and was losing, 4-2, when Brad Lidge, the Astros closer, came in to shut down the Cardinals in the ninth inning and blew away the first two batters he faced. Members of the Astros climbed to the top of their dugout, ready to rush the field in exultation. Then David Eckstein singled to left. Jim Edmonds walked. And Albert Pujols drove an 0-1 pitch deep to leftfield.

Lidge sank to a crouch, the crowd fell silent, Andy Pettitte mouthed the words, "Oh my", and the ball went over Minute Maid Park's limestone facade. The

OLDEST PLAYER TO HIT A HOME RUN

THE TOP SPOT on this list belongs to Jack Quinn, a pitcher who won 247 games in a 23-year career. Quinn was around so long that he was a teammate of both Wee Willie Keeler and, more than two decades later, Jimmie Foxx. Quinn was the oldest player in baseball in 1927, and he didn't retire for another six seasons. He hit the eighth and final home run of his career on June 27, 1930, when he was 46 years and 357 days old.

The no. 2 through no. 5 spots are all held by Julio Franco, who hit nine homers at the age of 46 in 2005. His last came on August 13, 10 days before his birthday and just two days shy of Quinn. So each time Franco, who's now with the Mets, goes deep in 2006, he will set a new record for senior citizen dingers.

CONTINUED ON PAGE 182

521
No. T15
WILLIE McCOVEY

534
No. 14
JIMMIE FOXX

521
No. T15
TED WILLIAMS

536*
No. T12
KEN GRIFFEY JR.

536
No. T12
MICKEY MANTLE

548
No. 11
MIKE SCHMIDT

563
No. 10
REGGIE JACKSON

573
No. 8
HARMON KILLEBREW

569*
No. 9
RAFAEL PALMEIRO

583
No. 7
MARK McGWIRE

MOST CAREER *Home Runs*

* STILL ACTIVE

512
No. T17
ERNIE BANKS

512
No. T17
EDDIE MATHEWS

511
No. 19
MEL OTT

504
No. 20
EDDIE MURRAY

755
No. 1
HANK AARON

714
No. 2
BABE RUTH

708*
No. 3
BARRY BONDS

588*
No. 5
SAMMY SOSA

586
No. 6
FRANK ROBINSON

660
No. 4
WILLIE MAYS

Cardinals, on the brink of extinction moments before, won, 5-4, and lived to fight another day.

It didn't really matter to Cardinals fans that the Astros won Game 6. Pujols' dinger was one of those moments that turned around the feeling of a series, even a season, and left Cardinals fans sated. Sure, nobody can summon bolts like that on demand. And when they don't come, we exhale and try our best to imitate the athletes who have to shake off failure, ignore bad omens, and start again. But when they do strike, they flash all the power of our collective longings.

After a season of dreadful revelations, Pujols reminded us all of a central truth: Home runs validate our most irrational hopes.

THE PAST AND THE FUTURE

AGE:

99

RAY BERRES

AGE:

98

BILLY WERBER

AGE:

21

PRINCE FIELDER

RAY BERRES, a catcher for four teams, was born in 1907 and hit three home runs in an 11-year career that ended in 1945. Billy Werber, who was born in 1908 and was the starting third baseman for the pennant-winning Reds of 1939 and 1940, had 78 career dingers. These gentlemen are the oldest living players to have gone yard.

Prince Fielder, whose father, Cecil, was a two-time AL home run champion and the only player to smack 50 or more taters in a season between 1977 and 1995, was the youngest player to homer in the major leagues in 2005. Prince was born in 1984 and will start at first base for Milwaukee in 2006; he has as good a chance as anyone to be baseball's next great slugger.

As I write these words,
Barry Bonds is getting ready to play
in 2006, needing just
47 home runs to break Hank Aaron's
career mark of 755 dingers.
Bonds currently ranks no. 3 on the
all-time list; the next-closest
active player, Sammy Sosa, trails him
by 120 homers.

BUT BONDS isn't the player with the best shot at passing Aaron. That distinction belongs to Alex Rodriguez, who is further away than Barry Lamar from the most important record in sports, but who's propelling himself toward his target with considerably more force.

How can we tell? By using a method Bill James called the Favorite Toy when he devised it back in the 1980s to estimate a player's chance of meeting a specific goal, in this case 756 home runs.

The central idea of the Favorite Toy is that distance equals velocity multiplied by time. Got it? Okay, so now you need three pieces of information about A-Rod and his pursuit of 756 home runs:

1. HR Needed: A-Rod had 429 career homers at the end of the 2005 season, which means he entered 2006 needing 327 more to get to 756.

2. Established HR Level: That's a weighted average to estimate the player's current level of performance. For 2006, this is found by adding the sum of three times his 2005 home run total, two times his 2004 homers, and his 2003 home runs, then dividing by 6. Rodriguez' Established HR Level is 43.8 homers per year, the highest in baseball.

3. Years Remaining: Calculate this by multiplying the player's age by 0.6 and subtracting the result from 24. A-Rod is 30. Subtract 18 (0.6 x 30) from 30 and you have 6—the number of years A-Rod has left in which he'll stay at his established HR level (43.8 per year).

Once this data is in hand, you can estimate how many home runs a player will hit in the remainder of his career by multiplying his established home run level by his years remaining. By this formula, A-Rod's got 263 dingers left in the tank.

The odds of reaching the goal are then estimated as the number of remaining home runs divided by the number of home runs needed, minus 0.5. For Rodriguez, this is (263/327) – 0.5, or 0.304. A-Rod has a 30.4 percent chance of breaking Aaron's record, which happens to be the highest figure in baseball.

According to this method, 17 players have a chance to hit 600 career home runs:

ALEX RODRIGUEZ STATS

Year	Team	G	R	HR	RBI	BB	AVG	OPS
1994	Mariners	17	4	0	2	3	.204	.445
1995	Mariners	48	15	5	19	6	.232	.672
1996	Mariners	146	141	36	123	59	.358	1.045
1997	Mariners	141	100	23	84	41	.300	.846
1998	Mariners	161	123	42	124	45	.310	.919
1999	Mariners	129	110	42	111	56	.285	.943
2000	Mariners	148	134	41	132	100	.316	1.026
2001	Rangers	162	133	52	135	75	.318	1.021
2002	Rangers	162	125	57	142	87	.300	1.015
2003	Rangers	161	124	47	118	87	.298	.995
2004	Yankees	155	112	36	106	80	.286	.888
2005	Yankees	162	124	48	130	91	.321	1.031
	Career Totals	1592	1245	429	1226	730	.307	.962

Sammy Sosa	97%	Andruw Jones	10%
Alex Rodriguez	89%	Adam Dunn	6%
Rafael Palmeiro	61%		
Ken Griffey Jr.	49%		
Manny Ramirez	44%		
Andruw Jones	41%		
Albert Pujols	41%		
Adam Dunn	26%		
Vladimir Guerrero	17%		
Mark Teixeira	16%		
David Ortiz	10%		
Derrek Lee	9%		
Miguel Cabrera	8%		
Paul Konerko	6%		
Carlos Delgado	3%		
Adrian Beltre	3%		
Aramis Ramirez	2%		

These are impressive odds, suggesting that five or so current major leaguers will join Bonds beyond the 600-homer mark. But most aren't likely to go too much further; only half a dozen players have an established chance at 700 home runs. And just five have established a chance to hit 756:

Alex Rodriguez	30%
Barry Bonds	28%
Albert Pujols	15%

This seems reasonable in light of Bonds' recent fragility—not to mention his oft stated intention to stop once he passes Babe Ruth. And it's one more example of how impressive Aaron's home run record is.

Even after a decade of hyperinflated home run totals, 755 has withstood challenges from sluggers such as Sosa and Palmeiro. And while you could not construct a better long-term hitting machine than the always-consistent A-Rod, he has less than a one in three chance of climbing past Aaron.

Whether he gets there round about 2014 or not, here's hoping Rodriguez loosens up a little along the way. He's been more attached in the popular imagination to the value of his contract than any slugger since Babe Ruth. Heading into 2006 with two well-deserved MVPs, it's time for A-Rod to take a page—not the whole book, just a page—from the carefree careers of Ruth and Jimmie Foxx and Mickey Mantle.

If A-Rod really wants to feel the love he's got to learn that fans like their home run kings to swing with joy.

ALEX RODRIGUEZ

In the Dugout

Dingers! is a book, and not a collection of stray thoughts rattling around my head about the Douglas Copper Kings of the Class C Arizona-Mexico League, because four people collaborated with me on it from first pitch to final out.

To say **Sam Eckersley** of SpotCo designed this book is a gross understatement. He understood what we needed even when I couldn't articulate it, he created an overall look that is both lively and elegant, and he built every page sketch by sketch.

Simon Brennan and **Doug Mittler** extended my research, came up with ideas, challenged my arguments, checked and re-checked every number and statement of fact, drafted four items in Chapters 1 and 2 when the project went into extra innings, and provided invaluable feedback all the way. And they did all this with unfailing good humor even when we were all exhausted. Any remaining misjudgments or omissions are my responsibility.

Glen Waggoner, who carries more baseball knowledge in his left pinky than most people will acquire in a lifetime, took my far-flung ideas and shaped them into a book. I have learned much from his deft editing and his professionalism.

Gary Hoenig, who somehow runs both ESPN Books and *ESPN The Magazine*, had the idea for this book and the confidence that I could write it.

More than a brilliant copy editor, **Beth Adelman** was a patient but firm guide who helped keep this project on the rails during the final, hectic days of its production.

Invaluable statistical research was provided by **Steve Hirdt** and the crew at the **Elias Sports Bureau**; by sabermetrician extraordinaire **David Vincent**; by **Claudette Burke** and **Jeremy Jones** of the National Baseball Hall of Fame; and by **Dr. Frederic Keating, John Manuel, Bob McConnell,**

Michael Walczak, and Bill Weiss.

At ESPN Books and *ESPN The Magazine*, thanks to Craig Winston for heroic work in overseeing the research effort; to Kristi Guerrero for wonderful photo research; to Nigel Goodman and Dale Brauner for helping secure reprint rights; and to Chris Raymond, Sandy DeShong, and Michael Solomon on the publishing side.

At SpotCo, the designs of Sam, Bashan Aquart, and Tzvetan Kostov challenged and inspired me to try to write words worthy of their efforts. Thanks also to Drew Hodges, Brian Berk, Gail Anderson, Dan Savage, Jessica Disbrow, Darren Cox, Gary Montalvo, Tom Greenwald, and Mary Littell.

I have never met Bill James, but a few months ago, I sent him an e-mail about home runs. He was kind enough to reply, which only encouraged me to send more questions. He answered all those, too. I thank him for his time, and for his endless zeal for researching ideas instead of accepting conventional wisdom, which has galvanized me ever since my friends Matt and Shane showed me a copy of his *Baseball Abstract*, a Rosetta stone for understanding baseball back in 1983.

The following friends and colleagues provided ideas, inspiration, and support: Shaun Assael, Gary Belsky, Walter Colleran, Rob Donlon, Charles Einstein, Neil Fine, Beverly Goodman, Patricia Keating, John Manuel, Duff McDonald, John McElhone, Linda McElhone, Amy Nelson, Jon Pessah, Richard Reeves, Andrew Ross, Sara Keating Ross, Sully Ross, Ellen Stark, John Underwood, and Perry Van Der Meer.

Finally, the love and forbearance of my wife, Karen Keating, and our daughter, Ellie, make possible everything I do.

—*Peter Keating* MONTCLAIR, N.J., March 2006

Photo Credits

Page 96 • Hank Aaron: *The Sporting News*/ZUMA Press
Page 185 • Alex Rodriguez: John Cordes/Icon SMI/ZUMA Press
Page 172 • Albert Pujols: Shaun Best/Reuters/Corbis
Page 144 • Mark McGwire: Jeff Haynes/AFP/Getty Images
Page 99 • Hank Greenberg: National Baseball Hall of
Fame Library/MLB Photos via Getty Images
Page 142 • Jim Rice: Rich Pilling/MLB Photos via Getty Images
Page 119 • Jimmy Wynn: Diamond Images/Getty Images
Page 94 • Rocky Colavito: *The Cleveland Plain Dealer*
Page 32 • Babe Ruth: National Baseball Hall of Fame
Library/MLB Photos via Getty Images
Page 61 • Mickey Mantle: Olen Collection/Diamond Images/Getty Images
Page 15 • Home Run Baker: The Sporting News/ZUMA Press
Page 169 • Barry Bonds: Paul Kitagaki Jr., *The Sacramento Bee*/ZUMA Press
Page 121 • Mike Schmidt: MLB Photos via Getty Images

Page 192 ILLUSTRATION • Mark Stutzman

Permissions

Page 30 • From the book *Guys, Dolls, and Curveballs: Damon Runyon on Baseball*,
Copyright © 2005, Appears by permission of the publisher,
Carroll & Graf, a division of Avalon Publishing Group, Inc.
Page 48 • From the article by John Carmichael, which has been reproduced in
this book with permission from the *Chicago Sun-Times*, Inc. All rights reserved.
Page 74 • "The Ballad of Rocky Nelson" by Raymond Souster is reprinted from
the *Collected Poems of Raymond Souster* by permission of Oberon Press.
Page 79 • From "Miracle of Coogan's Bluff" by Red Smith.
Originally published in the *New York Herald Tribune*.
Copyright © 1951 by The New York Times Co. Reprinted with permission.
Page 127 • From "How Life Imitates the World Series" by Thomas
Boswell, Copyright © 1982 by Washington Post Writer's Group. Used
by permission of Doubleday, a division of Random House, Inc.

Scorecard

"The hit and run, stolen base, bunt, and sacrifice are deteriorating from unuse and they only hit for their amusement and pleasure for the home run."

— *Ty Cobb*